Stenhouse Publishers
Portland, Maine

Dorothy
Barnhouse

READERS FRONT & CENTER

Helping All Students Engage with Complex Texts

Stenhouse Publishers
www.stenhouse.com

Credits
Frog and Toad Are Friends excerpts: Text copyright © 1970 Arnold Lobel. Illustrations copyright © 1970 Arnold Lobel. Used by permission of HarperCollins Publishers.

Library of Congress Cataloging-in-Publication Data
Barnhouse, Dorothy (Dorothy J.)
    Readers front & center : helping all students engage with complex texts/ Dorothy Barnhouse.
        pages cm
        ISBN 978-1-57110-967-5 (paperback)
        1. Reading comprehension. 2. Cognition in children—Study and teach-ing. 3. Reading (Elementary) 4. Reading (Middle school) I. Title. II. Title: Readers front and center.
        LB1050.45.B375 2014
        372.47—dc23
                                                                    2013048770

Cover design, interior design, and typesetting by Martha Drury
Manufactured in the United States of America

PRINTED ON 30% PCW
RECYCLED PAPER

20 19 18 17 16 15 14   9 8 7 6 5 4 3 2 1

For Nora, wherever you are.

CONTENTS

ACKNOWLEDGMENTS

This book began many years ago with a child—Nora—and I first want to thank her and the other students in the New York City Public Schools who show up (usually) and do what they're told (usually). We owe each of you so much more, and my deepest hope is that somewhere within the cracks of the system you'll find a few exhilarating moments, as I have in my teaching—as I did in my conversation with Nora—and that those moments will sustain you and help you create more exhilarating moments.

Nora's story could not have become the seed for a book without Maureen Barbieri, my editor. Maureen, guardian-angel-like, has a knack for popping into my life when I most need her. The first time was when I was learning how to teach reading after more than a decade of teaching writing. Maureen and I landed in the same school for a time and she often found me stumbling down the stairs at the end of the day, spent and despairing. Learning is hard! Maureen, knowing that a sit-down meal in the middle of a school day can be immensely healing for a teacher, invited me to join her once, then twice. Soon we had a regular table. Maureen added immeasurably to those meals, letting me unload without judgment and gently moving the talk to what really mattered—books we were reading. More than ten years later, there she was again, urging me forward, helping me trust myself, getting to what really matters. This book describes a kind of journey I didn't even know I was on, and Maureen has been there, bookending it. Thank you.

Thanks, too, to the Stenhouse team—patient, skilled, and invisibly working. Jill Cooley, Chris Downey, Rebecca Eaton, Jay Kilburn, and Anne Sauve have all had a hand in turning the words I typed on a screen into words bound in a real book. Imagine! Dan Tobin and Philippa Stratton believed in the content of the book, had faith in the outcome, and exhibited rare patience for the process.

While I don't name specific teachers in this book, I want to mention a few here from a few of the schools I work in on a regular basis.

First, Charlotte Butler, who coordinates literacy instruction in secondary schools in Aurora, Colorado, has served as an unfailing model for how to keep a district focused on students. Charlotte continually nourishes my faith in teaching teachers—and my hunger for good Mexican food.

At the Brooklyn School of Inquiry, Donna Taylor and Nicole Nelson thoughtfully lead a group of teachers dedicated to progressive education. Thanks to Nelsa Boyer-Madisson and Sevgi Unay for letting me loose with their students, and to Sara Inbar for the "Book/Brain" phrase.

PS 261 in Brooklyn has remained close to my heart and essential to my work for many years. I wish I could thank all thirty-two-plus teachers individually, for each of them—in a meeting, in a classroom demo, in a study group, in a quick conversation while passing in the hall—has sparked my thinking. Millie DeStefano, Melissa Farran, Lindsay Frey, Kelly Nowlin, and Nan O'Shea allowed me to try out specific ideas in their classrooms that I try to articulate in these pages; Mariel Casey thoughtfully "translated" the "Book/Brain" chart into a web for her students; and the entire second-grade team allowed me lots of time to try out small groups with their students. In addition, I continue to be inspired by the teaching of Megan Kane, Karen Kaz, Jamie Silberstein, and Colleen Torres. Never once have these teachers doubted that each of their students could do the big, complicated work of reading. That faith in students starts at the top, and so I thank Zipporiah Mills, Jackie Allen Joseph, and Sara Apfel for leading this extraordinary school, where standardization is never mistaken for standards and agency is the goal for every student.

Gary Fairweather, the principal at PS/MS 43 in Far Rockaway, Queens, afforded me the opportunity to work one-on-one with many teachers in many grades, as close as a consultant can get to having her own classroom. Special thanks to Christopher Allen, George Bombadier, Lorraine Bonilla, Regina Byrnes, Gayle Hamias, Danielle Hoffbauer, Petal Myrie, Tina D'Orsa, Vanessa Petroglia, and Sharon Sessing for sharing their students with me, and to the third-, fifth-, and sixth-grade teams for their willingness to jump headfirst into new ideas. I also want to appreciate the entire school community. Resilient and caring to begin with, the teachers and staff at this school became even more so in the aftermath of Hurricane Sandy. I came home every day after work to electricity and dry floors; many of them did not. For their courage and dedication, many, many thanks.

Storms of one kind or another are hitting teachers all over the country. And so it's to all of you whom I want to send my biggest thanks. Thank you for showing up, for listening to your students, for learning side by side with them each day. Quite simply, thank you for teaching. This book is a small attempt to cheer you on from the sidelines. I hope it helps.

It's easy to start a book but almost impossible to finish it. For helping me do the impossible, I have to thank my family: my husband, Jack, and our daughters, Lucy and Ella. As the months turned into a year and threatened to turn into another year, Jack began greeting me every evening with these inspiring words: "The End!" One day I joked, "The end of what? Our marriage?" Fortunately, it wasn't. For your patience with me through this process, thank you. Now, what's for dinner?

INTRODUCTION
Learning to Listen

We have two ears and only one tongue in order that we may hear more and speak less.

—Laertius

I am sitting down to write this at the same time that construction is starting in a vacant lot next to my apartment building. Gone are the usual sounds of urban Brooklyn wafting in from the backyards: the low hum of nearby traffic, an occasional horn or siren, birds, children, church bells, and ice cream trucks. Now, it's pumps and generators, pile drivers, cement mixers. A big building is going up and it's producing some big noise!

So it comes as no surprise that I've been thinking about noise a lot lately. My interest in noise was piqued when I heard an article on NPR—the volume of my radio turned up to maximum so I could hear above the din next door—about the impact of ocean noise on marine mammals. It seems that the noise humans are creating in the oceans—starting with propeller ships 150 years ago and continuing to today's use of air guns to explore for natural gas—interferes with marine mammals' abilities to hear and communicate with each other, which is severely impacting their survival (NPR Staff 2013).

Too much noise!

But even when the construction crew calls it a day and the quiet of evening settles over my neighborhood, there are other noises I face. My in-box beeps, my phone chirps. Blogs, Twitter, and all manner of newspapers and magazines form an endless stream of chatter about education, testing, and standards. Anyone with a device is chiming in, often with vitriol, about what is wrong with public schools and what can be done better. These voices are exhilarating and important. We need voices, and lots of them, to speak up about the state of our profession: the reforms that are not righting what is really wrong, the evaluations that are not valuing teachers, the tests that are eclipsing learning. But while the activist in me wants to raise my voice and join my colleagues in speaking loudly and frequently for what I feel is right and necessary in education, the teacher in me wants to unplug. Let me rephrase that: the teacher in me *needs* to unplug. Sometimes it all feels like too much noise, noise that is distracting rather than energizing, noise that takes me away from my work rather than helping me focus. I feel the need to do what so many teachers tell me they have done during previous shifts in educational policies: they shut their doors and pay attention to what they know is most important—the students in front of them.

I say this with some trepidation. Up until now, my job has consisted mostly of urging teachers to open their doors. Collaboration and public learning—signified by open doors—should be the DNA of schools. Additionally, I don't have my own classroom. Instead, I travel from room to room, building to building, city to city. I depend on teachers opening their doors to me so we can work together toward better practice.

And yet.

That open door can often let in a deafening cacophony. Randy Bomer calls such noise a "policy churn" (Bomer 2011, 6), a term I love because it evokes those propellers that have been preventing whales from hearing each other for over a century. I know there is policy churn when I walk into classrooms and hear teachers ask questions that begin: "Am I supposed to?" "Am I allowed to?" "Should I?" or "Is it OK if I?" The chatter of mandates—lists of grade-level texts provided by the authors of the Common Core State Standards (CCSS), a publisher's interpretation of those books, an outside curriculum promising alignment with standardized tests, the threat of evaluations based on those test scores—has taken the place of the voices of the students sitting in front of these teachers. We have been deafened by policy churn.

It is clearly time to close our doors.

We need to shut off the noise that seeps into our classrooms so we can better listen to our students. Listening is hard for most of us, but especially,

I think, for those of us who teach. Talking seems to be a requirement of our profession, practically a synonym for teaching. But listening?

When I think about the kind of listening that happens in schools, I think of how we, as teachers, usually listen *for*. We listen for the right answers, the key words, the idea that best matches the tests or what we're thinking. This is most obviously evident when we hear ourselves asking questions and replying to a student's answer by saying, "OK, but I'm thinking of something else." Though most of us have moved away from the guess-what's-on-the-teacher's-mind method of teaching, we still fall into this trap, perhaps using more subtle language. I'm thinking of how often during discussions I say, "Yes, and what else?" Am I honestly asking students to add to their thinking or am I listening for something that matches the "it" I want them to get?

There is no doubt that we are teaching at a time when success is determined by whether our students can "get" the "it"—and get it in specified texts. Answers, unfortunately, seem to matter more than questions these days, and assessments are overshadowing learning. Thomas Newkirk puts it this way in his marvelous book *The Art of Slow Reading*: "The test, rather than being built on a value system, becomes the value system" (Newkirk 2011, 12).

But that's not to say we have to give in and teach toward these tests. Instead of listening *for* answers, we should be trying to listen to our students. I first wrote about the distinction between listening *for* and listening *to* with Vicki Vinton in our coauthored book, *What Readers Really Do* (Barnhouse and Vinton 2012). In the pages of *Readers Front and Center*, I'll be attempting to dig into that idea more deeply, to examine the implications of teaching—and specifically, teaching reading—that has, at its heart, listening.

A recent article in the *New Yorker* addresses this very issue, albeit in a different context. The writer, Atul Gawande, who has previously written about coaching and teaching, here describes efforts on the part of the Indian government and several nonprofit organizations to instill safer childbirth practices in some of that country's poorest villages. The practices seemed simple—better hand washing, for example, to prevent infection, and swaddling the infant next to the mother's skin to prevent hypothermia—yet the birth attendants were not internalizing these practices and babies continued to die shortly after birth. It was only when training nurses spent time on the ground, side by side with the birth attendants, talking over tea, listening to why they were doing or not doing what they should, that practices began to change. When Gawande interviewed a birth attendant about why she finally did change her practices, she responded that the training nurse "was nice" and "smiled a lot" and that talking with her "wasn't like talking to someone who was trying to find mistakes . . . . It was like talking to a friend" (Gawande 2013, 45). That's what it took to make changes in practice: smiling, talking, being a friend. In contrast, countries that implemented similar health-care training programs "at arm's length, going 'low touch,' without sandals on the ground . . . have failed almost entirely. People talking to people is still how the world's standards change" (44).

We can't teach people if we don't know them and we can't know them if we don't listen to them.

Teaching as listening is not a new concept. Most famously, Don Graves made listening the core of his teaching. He listened to students and taught them, in turn, to listen to each other (Graves 1994). But listening is a concept that seems to have gotten shuffled to the bottom of the deck in recent years. I think, for example, of the entire movement toward national standards, a movement that was created by a small group of people with limited public input and discussion (Newkirk 2013). I also think of the scripted curricula that are being offered to schools and districts in the name of helping teachers help their students "meet" the Common Core State Standards. These curricula come loaded with questions teachers are supposed to ask and possible answers they should be listening *for* ("Guide students to recognize," "Help students identify," "Possible responses include," and "Sentence starters are").

As a result of such teaching, I'm afraid, students are being trained to think of reading as a listening-*for* activity rather than learning to listen to the texts in front of them. Tom Newkirk describes such readers as those for whom "the text has no hold" (Newkirk 2011, 50). He, too, recognizes this as a kind of hearing loss, realizing that in addition to visualizing, readers "auditorize" or "hear" the "way writing is told" (50). While some readers seem to develop and practice auditorizing as they read silently to themselves, some readers—nonreaders really—do not. These readers, Newkirk states, need to develop an "inner ear" that allows them to "hear" the print their eyes take in (50).

Teaching in a way that suggests that texts have answers is exactly the opposite of what these students need. They will read in order not to dwell in a text but to hunt and peck for an answer, which they can then deliver to their teacher. I see this all the time in classrooms. In a high school English class reading *The Road* by Cormac McCarthy, for example, students were discussing a particular scene in small groups—a scene none of them had bothered to read for homework. One "smart" reader had it all figured out, however. "Just read the back, guys," he advised his group. "It's a post-apocalyptic novel. That means it's about hope and despair, so the dog here probably symbolizes hope." Satisfied, the students shut their books and wrote their exit slips. Done. I also see this in classrooms of younger students who are told to use specific "strategies" to "identify" themes or main ideas. They skim through a book looking for the answers: the first sentence of a paragraph in expository writing, for example, or in narrative, the place where an "elder" might teach a "youth" a lesson. These students have been trained well—to listen *for*, not *to*.

And though the Common Core State Standards were written purportedly to facilitate deeper thinking than these scenarios suggest, the reality is not quite so rosy. In fact, as the texts used in classrooms become more challenging and the curricula more narrow, students seem more rather than less likely to become disengaged answer seekers. History has shown this to be true. As choice and independence have been replaced by requirements and struggle, "optimum learning" has gone down (Allington 2001, 46). Stephen Krashen's research would seem to confirm this as well. He notes that language and literacy learning occur when messages are understood. If the messages are not interesting ("compelling" says Krashen), or are so far out of reach that they cause high anxiety, low self-esteem, and lack of motivation, then learning does not take place (Krashen 2004).

I believe this is likely to continue happening as the CCSS become more deeply embedded in schools. This is because Standards 1 through 9, which describe skills such as inferring, analyzing, interpreting, and evaluating, are followed by what I think is the very problematic Standard 10. Those of you familiar with this standard know it's the one that states, "Read and comprehend complex literary and informational texts independently and proficiently" (Common Core State Standards Initiative 2012c).

On the face of it, it's not much. But look at those words: *comprehend, complex,* and *independently and proficiently*. Think about what each of those words mean. First, *comprehend*—a whole industry has sprouted up around what it means to comprehend. As for *complex*, that's a relative term—what is complex for one person might not be for another. And then there's *independently and proficiently*. What, exactly, does that look like and how can teachers tell whether students are doing complex comprehension well and doing so on their own?

The authors of the CCSS, perhaps anticipating issues regarding Standard 10, wrapped several appendices around it that attempt to clarify why text complexity matters and how to determine the complexity of a text. I have no issue with the rationale behind the need for text complexity. By definition, education is a process of teaching students to think in increasingly complex ways about increasingly complex texts, whatever those texts may be: books, numbers, molecules, music.

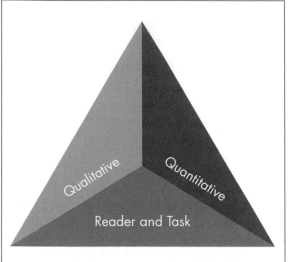

Qualitative

Quantitative

Reader and Task

Figure 1
The three
factors used to
measure text
complexity in
the Common
Core State
Standards

What I have trouble with is the way in which text complexity has been measured and rolled out for use in schools. The authors of the standards measure the complexity of a text using three strands: quantitative factors, qualitative factors, and factors regarding the reader and the task (see Figure 1).

Quantitative measures include the length of words and sentences—those aspects of a text "better measured by algorithm than a human reader." Qualitative measures are those "only measurable by an attentive human reader," and include meaning, purpose, and structure. Texts that explicitly state their point, for example, will be less complex qualitatively than those that implicitly show it; texts that require a lot of background knowledge will be more complex than those that explain background within the text. And finally, Reader and Task measures take into account an individual reader's motivation, purpose, knowledge, and experience. Here, educators are expected to "employ professional judgment to match texts to particular students and tasks" (Common Core State Standards Initiative 2012a, 7).

But here is where practice has not matched theory. Although the diagram in Appendix A shows the "Reader and Task" at the base of the pyramid, the reality in classrooms is that the role of students and teachers has been marginalized. Classrooms all over the country are bursting with boxes of curricular materials filled with "Common-Core-aligned" texts, none of which the teachers were asked to professionally judge or match with any of their students. I believe this is because side by side with Appendix A is Appendix B, the place where "text exemplars" are listed. These are texts that have been determined by the authors of the Common Core "to exemplify the level of text complexity and quality that the Standards require all students in a given grade band to engage with" (Common Core State Standards Initiative 2012b, 2). The word *all* is a tell here. These are not texts that have been matched to "particular" students. These are not suggestions. *All* students are being *required* to read texts like these. That means the Qualitative and Quantitative criteria have trumped the Reader and Task criteria. So much for being at the base of the pyramid.

So what? Why does this matter?

Well, here's why this matters: An eighth-grade boy has finished with a task the rest of his class is still working on. Following his teacher's instructions to read independently when finished, he has taken out the "Common Core-aligned" textbook recently acquired by his school and the only book available in the room for "independent reading." He sits for about ten minutes with the book open to an excerpted chapter from *The Adventures of Tom Sawyer*, one of the exemplars from Appendix B for Grades 6–8.

Here are the first few sentences of the excerpt, which is the opening of Chapter 31 in the real book:

> *Now to return to Tom and Becky's share in the picnic. They tripped along the murky aisles with the rest of the company, visiting the familiar wonders of the cave—wonders dubbed with rather over-descriptive names, such as "The Drawing Room," "The Cathedral," "Aladdin's Palace," and so on. Presently the hide-and-seek frolicking began, and Tom and Becky engaged in it with zeal until the exertion began to grow a trifle wearisome; then they wandered down the sinuous avenue holding their candles aloft and reading the tangled webwork of names, dates, post-office addresses, and mottoes with which the rocky walls had been frescoed (in candle smoke). Still drifting along and talking, they scarcely noticed that they were now in a part of the cave whose walls were not frescoed. They smoked their own names under an overhanging shelf and moved on.* (Twain 1998, 159)

I approach the student and start talking to him about what he's reading. He (courageously) admits that he doesn't have a clue about what's going on in these sentences. I can see why, or at least some of why: there's the first and most obvious fact that this is written in a different era—the sentences are long, the paragraph itself is an unending block of text running down the page, and the language is not contemporary. Additionally, the reader—any reader—has no context for these sentences. It is clear from the first sentence (*Now to return to Tom and Becky's share in the picnic*) that this is an excerpt. In the previous chapter, which does not appear in this school's textbook, Twain has generously described the cave in which Tom and Becky find themselves and explicitly given information that would help a reader make sense of some details that appear here: *the rest of the company*, for example, or *the familiar wonders of the cave*. In addition, the previous chapter has explained that Becky and Tom have gone missing and that a search party has been sent out to the cave to find them.

But does this boy know this? No. For how could he? That chapter is not here. This is a text without a context. And while those previous details are certainly not essential to comprehend exactly what's going on in these first few sentences, they would certainly be clues that any reader would rely on to ground themselves in this scene, in other words, to get that Tom and Becky are in a cave, exploring, and on the brink of getting lost.

And so when I ask this boy what he thinks might be going on in this paragraph, he takes a stab at it and says he thinks that Tom and Becky may be in a movie theater. When I ask him what makes him think that, he points to the words *aisle* and *dubbed* and to the clue about Aladdin, which he says he knows is a movie. At this point the bell rings. The boy, I'm quite sure, feels saved; he scoops up his belongings, leaving the book open on the desk behind him. I linger with the text a little longer and can't help but wonder what he might have made out of the passage about the characters smoking their names under a shelf.

This is a text exemplar, all right—an example of how *not* to use texts in classrooms. Disembodied. For assessment purposes only. Matched to the Qualitative and Quantitative criteria laid out in Appendix A, but certainly not to that of the Reader and Task.

What's wrong with this picture is that the teacher has been rendered powerless. She was handed a textbook and told to use it. She was not required to employ any "professional judgment, experience, or knowledge" except how to manage a classroom in which a few students may finish a task before the others. As a result the student has been rendered powerless. Just as the chapter from Tom Sawyer has been yanked out of its context and placed, absurdly, in this textbook, so the act of reading has been yanked out of its context. There is no *why*, as in why should this student read this particular text; there is no *how*, as in how should this student read this particular text; and there is no *so what*, as in what's the payoff for this student's efforts. The Reader and the Task don't matter at all in this scenario.

We have to right that wrong. Our students need to become the center of our teaching—not the texts, not the standards, and certainly not the assessments.

To start, let's visualize a different diagram about text complexity. Instead of the pyramid that appears in Appendix A, let's think of a pebble thrown into a pond. The pebble is the student and the pond is the text. When that pebble hits the surface of the pond, we see ripples. That's the thinking the student is doing as he reads. By paying attention to those ripples—and doing so by listening *to* the student—we can get a better understanding of how that text might be complex for that student. There may be some quantitative issues—there are definitely a lot of big words and long sentences in that

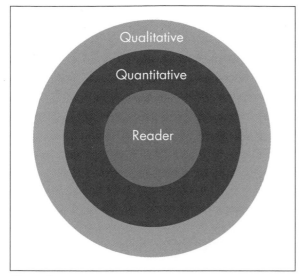

Figure 2
The reader is at the center of what makes a text complex.

excerpt from Tom Sawyer. There may be some qualitative issues—how much background knowledge is necessary for an urban teenager to fill in the missing context? And there may also be some task issues—why should this student bother to read this text? But not every student will be confronted by each and every one of these issues in the same way. One student may comprehend the difficult words in context; another may read on and discover more clues about a cave and therefore revise his initial ideas about the movie theater. As teachers that's what we need to see—our students interacting with texts. That's where our teaching needs to start. Figure 2 is a revisualization of what this kind of thinking about text complexity could look like instead of the pyramid.

Whether the Common Core becomes just another policy churn or grows into the backbone of this country's curriculum for decades to come, I hope we can learn this much from the conversations it has sparked: We cannot say one thing and do another. We cannot say that students are an important factor in determining text complexity and then create curricula that ignore students. We cannot say that students need to read independently and proficiently and then hand them texts they can't read.

Our methods have to match our goals. How we teach is of equal if not greater importance than what we teach. We know this because we know that "language is not merely representational . . . but constitutive." It "creates realities and invites identities" (Johnston 2004, 9). To do right by our students—whether it is to make sure they are college- and career-ready or ready for duties that surpass college and careers, such as building and developing relationships and living actively in a community in which they feel a sense of mutual and shared responsibility—we need to make sure that we are inviting them to take on a lifetime of learning. This means treating them like learners, placing them in the center of our classrooms, and doing so not in word but in deed. Only then will they develop agency and engagement and only then will they truly be "independent and proficient."

This book is an attempt to help teachers help their students take on identities as learners. To start, we need to put students front and center in our classrooms and we need to listen to them. The first three chapters of this book are about conducting reading conferences that allow us to truly teach from where our students are, first by listening to their thinking as they read and then rooting them in their own agency as learners. The following three chapters are a guide to stepping students up from where they are so they can think more complexly in more complex texts—not because they have to, but because they can and because they want to.

NOTICING SMARTER
Researching What We Don't Know

To pay attention is our endless and proper work.

—Maxine Greene

If you're anything like me, you learned how to do reading conferences on the job: plunked down in the middle of a classroom full of students working—or not, as the case may be. Your brain was whirring: What should I say? What should I teach? And what should I do with the other twenty-nine kids staring at me as I make my way through the room?

And if you're anything like me, your first forays into reading conferences sounded something like this:

DB: So, what are you reading?
Student: [Shows the cover.]
DB: OK. So tell me about a little bit about it.
Student: [Starts to rehash the plot.]

DB: [Nods then becomes distracted by an outburst at another table; stands up and says, "Quiet please"; returns attention to the student.] Sorry. And then what happened?

Student: [Continues to rehash the plot, with a subplot now brought in.]

DB: [Glances at the back jacket to check whether the student is getting it right, glances at the clock.] Umm. So do you have any predictions about what might happen next?

Student: [Mumbles something that sounds like a prediction.]

DB: OK, then. Good work. Keep reading to see if you're right. [Suddenly remembers that a conference is supposed to sound like a conversation.] Oh, and ummm, are you liking the book? [Looks at the clock, snaps fingers frantically at the unruly table.] Good. Would you recommend it to a classmate? Good. You might want to write something up about it after you're done.

Student: [Gives a slight nod but maybe it's a shrug.]

OK, I exaggerate a little but maybe only a little and to make a point: If you're anything like me you find conferring with students around reading to be really, really hard. Even after studying and practicing conferring for years, it's still really, really hard. I'm going into a school tomorrow where eight teachers will be watching me conduct reading conferences, trying to learn from me. They'll most definitely want to know what to do and what to say. You probably have the same questions.

Here's my answer: I don't know.

Now if you're anything like me, saying, "I don't know" is really, really hard. Perhaps it's hard for everyone but my hunch is that it's hardest for teachers. We're paid to know and to pass on that knowledge. And *I'm* paid to teach teachers. I'm *really* supposed to know.

But that thinking has led me to make some of my biggest mistakes, especially about reading conferences. I look back on my early reading conferences and see as plain as day how trapped I was by "supposed-to-know" thinking: I was supposed to know about the book that the student was reading; I was supposed to know what that student needed at the moment; I was supposed to know how to teach whatever it was in that moment.

And the reason I was such a failure at those reading conferences is because that stance was a false one. *I didn't know*. I didn't know about the book; I didn't know what to teach; and I certainly didn't know *how* to teach it. But I couldn't admit that—to myself, to the teachers I worked with, or to my students. Ironically, it was only when I was finally able to admit that I *didn't* know that I was finally able to make sense of how to confer with readers. This is because I was finally able to step aside and listen.

What We Don't Know

So that's where we need to start: with what we don't know. The fact is, when we sit down to confer with a student we don't know anything. There is a book and there is a mind, and what is transpiring between the two is largely invisible to us. This isn't new thinking. In fact, many teachers acknowledge this and create artifacts that attempt to make comprehension visible—hence the evolution of reading responses and literary essays. Although writing about reading has its place in classrooms to be sure, it illuminates some things but not others. It can illuminate thoughts but not thinking; it can illuminate meaning but not how that meaning has been constructed. This is not just a rhetorical point. I believe that teachers can't truly teach reading until we understand *how* our students are arriving at meaning, a concept I explore with Vicki Vinton in *What Readers Really Do* (Barnhouse and Vinton 2012). Reading is a process of thinking—it is not just the thoughts themselves—and the invisible work of reading is how a mind takes words on a page and transforms them into meaning. The meaning itself is important, yes, but in classrooms where our job is to teach students *how* to read not *what* to read, the process by which that meaning has been made is vital to understand and to teach toward.

And we don't know that process. In fact we can't know that process unless we first admit that we don't know it. Not knowing is the point. As I approach a student during a reading conference, I can only begin to know what that student is thinking by shifting my attitude from the teacher who is supposed to know to the teacher who is supposed to discover. My primary job in a reading conference, therefore, is to get out of the way so I can listen, carefully, from a stance of not knowing. Only then will I truly be able to see a mind at work.

When we can catch a student's thinking in midswing—on the page, in the midst of all those words—we can glimpse how meaning is being constructed; we can see the invisible work of reading unique to each reader. Then we can move from not knowing to knowing. But to do so we first have to make students' thinking visible as they read, approaching them as seekers of information, as researchers. And like all researchers—whether in the field of humanities or sciences, whether formal or informal—we need to start our work with questions, something we want to know. The scientist noting the growth of an organism in a petri dish wants to know what makes it multiply; the child pushing a toy car back and forth, watching intently, wants to know how it moves. Teachers need to ask themselves what the mind work is that students are doing as they read. What kinds of thinking are they doing? How are they making meaning from the marks on the page in front of them?

Lucy Calkins, in her work on conferring in both reading and writing, has articulated three components in a conference: research, decide, and teach (Calkins 1994, 2001). The *research* component is where the teacher attempts "to learn where the child is as a reader and understand the child's intention" (Calkins 2001, 102). This is then followed by a *decision* about what to teach, and then the actual *teaching* moment. Working from this structure of *research, decide*, and *teach* has informed all of my conferring work, yet I have to confess that swiftly moving through all three components in one sitting fills me with anxiety—and usually a grim sense of failure. If I manage to research well enough to come to a smart decision about what to teach, then I don't usually have time to teach well. If I come to a decision about what to teach and teach it well, I'm often left with a nagging doubt that I didn't research well enough and perhaps the child needed something different at the time.

I would have persisted in thinking of this as a personal failing if I had not been introduced to Peter Johnston's book, *Choice Words* (2004). In it, he describes the act of noticing and naming, and articulates how vital it is in teaching. "Through our noticing and naming language," he writes, "children learn the significant features of the world, themselves and others" (20). Noticing and naming what students do as readers and writers, he argues, brings about an awareness of the thinking work involved, what it looks, sounds, and feels like, and even what it means to be a reader and a writer.

Reading those words and examples of noticing and naming from Johnston's book reminded me of the *research* component of a conference— but with a difference. Here, Johnston was showing that *noticing* wasn't just a preliminary quickstep on the way to a teaching point but was an essential part of a teaching mechanism in and of itself. I decided if Peter Johnston could do it, I could do it, and allowed myself to slow down my conferences—to see what I could notice and perhaps eventually name. This book is a product of that work, of slowing down each of the components of a conference—*research, decide*, and *teach*—in order to do all three better, or at least try to do them better.

But much of what happens in schools conspires against anything slow. The clock is often our worst enemy, looming as a scold to hurry up and teach already. Mandated tests are at the heart of that pressure, of course, providing a countdown we can't ignore. Most people I work with in schools understand that time and tests are necessary distractions—necessary because they are not going away, and distractions because they are not really at the heart of what our purpose is as educators. Our job is to teach students how and why to live literate lives, and we therefore need to allow students time to interact with print, time to practice, and time to develop a relationship with books.

Conferences are our indispensable partners in this journey. A conference is essentially an invitation to glimpse the intersection between a student and a text. What is this student doing and thinking as she reads? How can I know? This is the purpose of our conferring time—to create, sustain, and teach from these moments. But too often we lose sight of this purpose. We are told in direct and indirect ways that we have to cover rather than uncover material, talk rather than listen. The know-and-tell teacher inside each of us steps forward and replaces the researcher, the discoverer, the one who doesn't know—yet.

What We Can Know

When we embrace what we don't know, we can actually learn a lot and teach better as a result.

To illustrate, let me take you inside a conference I had with an eighth-grade student, Abby. Abby was reading a book I happened to have read, and as I sat down with her, she started talking about the book. She summarized the plot beautifully, had some insight into the main character, and had a theory about the title that hinted at an understanding of some of the themes at play in the book. I was impressed. She seemed like a wonderful reader. But I noticed something as she spoke. I noticed that she kept her book firmly closed. As she was speaking about the main character, she pointed to the illustration on the front cover; as she was speaking about the plot, she flipped the book over and pointed to the blurb on the back jacket.

I became curious. Why was she doing this? How did such sophisticated talk fit with such unsophisticated behavior? I didn't know and needed to find out. I asked Abby to open the book and read a little from where she left off. She obliged, found her place, and began to read beautifully. Again, I was impressed, but in the paragraphs she read there was an odd phrase the character had used. I wondered what she thought of it. "Why do you think the character said that?" I asked, pointing to the line. Abby was silent, staring at the page.

Perhaps reading out loud had hindered her comprehension, perhaps she had been focusing so much on fluency that she wasn't paying attention to meaning. I told her to take a minute and reread the section to herself. She did and then I asked again, "I'm curious about what you think the character is doing here?" She was again silent. I became more perplexed. "What do you think is happening on this page?" I finally asked. Abby shrugged.

The outcome of this conference is not that different from the one I described at the opening of this chapter: I didn't teach anything, and a student shrugged. Yet I ended up learning a whole lot more about this student than I did about the student in the first conference. I was able to do so because I moved from a supposed-to-know stance to one of not-knowing.

Initially, as Abby talked about the book, I held her comprehension up against my memory of the book—what I knew—and because they matched, I thought her comprehension was just fine. Clearly I was wrong. I had fallen into the trap of believing that if a student retells a story, that means they are "getting it." In fact, retelling—and the ability to retell—is complicated and has many subskills (and with SparkNotes and similar programs available on every student's smart phone, many opportunities for faking it). Readers need to think about chronology and cause and effect, for example; they need to accumulate details to see how these contribute to important ideas. But I had not glimpsed this or any other thinking Abby might have been doing because I was paying attention only to what she knew vis-à-vis what I knew. It was only when I stopped myself and wondered about something I didn't know—how someone could talk so dazzlingly about the book but keep it so firmly shut—that I got insight into her thinking. Her behavior piqued my curiosity and reminded me to ask genuine questions, questions I didn't know the answers to.

This can happen in many other scenarios as well. For example, in the course of a conference I might ask a student who the main character is in the book she's reading. If she provides me with an answer that I know to be incorrect, I may decide to teach her, then and there, how to identify a main character in a narrative. If I pause, however, and shift my thinking from one of knowing to one of not knowing, I may instead ask her why she thinks that character is the main character. She may respond by saying that this character is the one causing the problem, or this character is the one telling the story, or this character is the one she most identifies with, or this is the character on this page, or this is the character with a name she can pronounce. Each of those answers, of course, would give me different information about how this student is taking in a text and each would require me to teach something different.

With Abby, I didn't see her brain at work until I noticed something that made me curious and followed a line of questioning from there. Once I got her into the text I was able to ask her more questions I didn't know the answers to—why she thought a character said something and what she thought was going on in the scene. Only then did I arrive at the intersection of her mind and the text and see her thinking—or lack thereof.

Noticing What There Is to Be Noticed

When we accept the invitation to notice in our reading conferences, there is much to notice—and therefore much to potentially teach from. Some things are easily noticed because they are readily apparent. Fluency is one of these: inflection, tone, hesitation, self-correction, and pauses. Behavior is also usually visible. We can learn a lot about a reader if we watch: How do they find their place? How do they skim and flip through pages? Do they start reading the first word on a page even if it's in the middle of a sentence? Do they use their fingers as they read? Do they point to the picture or the cover or the blurb as they speak? In Abby's case, I noticed her handling of the book.

But there are also less visible aspects of reading that we need to take the time to notice: how students know what they know on a page; what textual clues contribute to their understanding; how they hold on to details from previous pages or chapters; how they are fitting parts together into a whole. We can notice how a student is literally and inferentially comprehending a page of text as well as how they might be constructing thematic understandings and how rigid or flexible they are as they do so.

But to notice anything, even the most visible—let alone invisible— aspects of reading, we have to set ourselves up to notice, we have to create the opportunity. So how do we do that? To answer that, let's look at a transcript from a conference I conducted with a fifth-grade student, Nora, who was reading *Loser* by Jerry Spinelli, a book I had not read at the time.

DB: Hi Nora, I'd like to get an idea of what you're thinking as you read, so can you read a short part of your book, from the page you're on now? Then I'll ask you some questions about what you're thinking.

Nora: OK. [Reads the following out loud.]

The first house has a slot. Donald slips a letter through. He listens for it to land but he cannot hear it. The slot is eye-high. Quietly, with his finger, he pushes in the swinging brass flap. He takes off his helmet and scrunches his eyeball to the slot and strains to see the letter on the floor. All he can make out is a green carpet. He looks around some more, hoping to spot something interesting, but all he sees is an ordinary living room with furniture and a picture on the wall of four basset hounds playing cards.

"No peeking!"

His father's voice pierces the jungle cat grumble of Clunker Four, prowling slowly along in the street. Donald lets the brass flapper swing down. He replaces his helmet and goes back to work. (Spinelli 2002, 66)

DB: OK, you can stop there. What is going on here?

Nora: He's helping his dad with his job.

DB: And who's the "he" you're talking about?

Nora: Donald.

DB: Donald. And what's his dad's job?

Nora: He's a mailman.

DB: Oh, so Donald is helping his dad deliver mail?

Nora: Yeah.

DB: It says here, *he takes off his helmet.* What's that about?

Nora: He's wearing a helmet.

DB: To deliver the mail?

Nora: It's a helmet his dad gave him. A mail helmet.

DB: A mail helmet? It doesn't say that here. How do you know that? Where did you get that information?

Nora: Over here. [Flips to previous page, skims a little, finds a section, and points to it. It reads: *He reaches into the backseat and pulls out a hat. And not just any hat. His own mail carrier hat. The postal blue, strawlike pith helmet that he wears on hot summer days with his Bermuda shorts uniform.*]

DB: Oh, I see. That's good work you're doing, carrying information in your head from the page before. And can you explain this sentence here [Points to *His father's voice pierced the jungle cat grumble . . . .*]. I don't understand that sentence. What do you make of it?

Nora: [Silent.]

DB: What's the *jungle cat grumble*?

Nora: [Rereads sentence to herself.] I think it's a cat.

DB: So you're rereading to try to figure it out. That's a great strategy. What makes you think it's a cat?

Nora: [Looks at me with a "duh" expression on her face.] Because it says *cat.*

DB: [Laughs.] Yes, it does indeed. OK then. How about *Clunker Four*? What do you think that means?

Nora: [Hesitates.] Is it a place?

DB: Why do you think it might be a place?

Nora: It's capitalized?

DB: Oh. So you know that the names of places are often capitalized and you're noticing that this is capitalized. But still it seems you're not sure, because you're asking me. The sentence is really confusing, right? Let's try to make sense of it by breaking it down and looking at it from the beginning. When it says, *His father's voice*, do we know whose voice the narrator is referring to?

Nora: Donald's?

DB: OK, how do you know that?

Nora: Andrew's?

DB: Oh, you're changing your mind. How come? What information in the text is telling you it could be Andrew's father's voice—or maybe Donald's?

Nora: [Silent.]

I'll reveal the outcome of this conference in Chapter 3 (spoiler alert: it did not end in a shrug), but first let's look at what I had to do to get into and stay in the noticing mode as I conferred:

- I stayed with a very small section of the text, only a few paragraphs really. I want to research the student, not the book, so I avoided a plot summary. A small section of text can provide a microcosm of larger thinking.
- I read along with Nora. A reader can tell a lot about a book from one page. And though there was much I didn't understand about the passage since I hadn't read the book, I did know, because I know how texts generally work, that *Clunker Four* was probably not being mentioned on page 66 for the first time and that there was probably an earlier reference to it, just as there was an earlier reference to the fact that this was a mail helmet Donald was wearing.
- I started with an open-ended question ("What's going on here?") but asked follow-up questions that quickly narrowed the field of vision ("What made you think that?" or "How do you know?"). If Nora had launched into a plot summary in response to my opening question, I would have tried to steer her back to the page she had just read. This is because I want to see what textual clues a reader uses to make literal and inferential sense of a scene. Since there was nothing in the words Nora had read about anything related to mail delivery, asking her how she knew the helmet was a mail helmet required her to demonstrate how she was carrying information from previous pages. Asking students

to show us how they got their thinking is also especially valuable if there is any kind of inferential thinking required on the page—and by inference, I mean anything that isn't explicitly stated. For example, the author doesn't come right out and tell us who is speaking the words *"No peeking,"* so a reader needs to infer that information. The author also doesn't come right out and tell us how Donald is feeling as he does what he does, or even why he is doing it. That is a different kind of inference a reader needs to make in order to comprehend this passage—and certainly something I could have explored with Nora, though the conference led me in a different direction.

- I noticed Nora's fluency and intonation but did not interrupt my research to teach from there. She actually read the sentence *His father's voice pierces the jungle cat grumble of Clunker Four, prowling slowly along in the street* with a slight pause after the word *jungle* as if *His father's voice pierces the jungle* was a sentence all to itself. That was a clue to me to ask further questions about her comprehension of that passage—not to correct her but to research her. Fluency is a visible manifestation of reading but much lies beneath, invisible, and I want to probe that through my research rather than staying on the surface.

- While I was constantly assessing Nora, I avoided evaluating her, neither praising her correct answers nor correcting her incorrect answers. When I asked her whose father's voice the text was referring to in the line *His father's voice* and she said, "Donald's," I was almost going to say, "Yes, you're right!" Because I didn't and instead asked, "How do you know that?" she revealed (by saying, "Andrew's") that she was not following textual clues on the page at all but grabbing at random answers.

And now for my confession: doing all of this took a great force of will on my part. No one loves to know-and-tell more than I do, and I had to stay in research mode with awareness and intention. I did so by constantly focusing on a question: What can I find out about this student as a reader? Every time I was tempted to start teaching, I reminded myself that my job at that moment was to explore that question.

One thing that made my job a little easier was the fact that I hadn't read the book. I had no clue about what was going on in the passage Nora read, so my opening question—"Tell me what's going on in this scene?"—was genuine. Many teachers feel that not knowing a book is the number one impediment to a successful reading conference. Over and over, teachers ask me, "How can I talk to a student about a book if I haven't read it?" And yet in Nora's case, not knowing the book helped me stay in the research mode.

Instead of holding her answers up against my own, which I did with Abby, who was reading a book I did know, I was able to ask questions such as, "How do you know that?" or "Where did you get that information?" I was able, then, to see Nora's mind at work.

Getting a glimpse of Nora's thinking in those first moments of the conference—seeing how she was accumulating information received on previous pages and using it to make sense of what she was currently reading—helped me get a glimpse of all there was to notice. This helped me trust this research mode and enabled me to stay in that mode even when her comprehension broke down—when she couldn't determine who the *his* was referring to in the phrase *His father's voice* and misinterpreted *jungle cat grumble* to mean there was a cat in the scene.

When students miscomprehend, my know-and-tell self loves to step forward and save the day. Perhaps I could tell Nora how to follow an antecedent to a pronoun; perhaps I could tell her what a clunker was; perhaps I could remind her of some lessons on figurative language her teacher had taught not too long ago; or I could steer her to self-correct by asking her something like, "Are you sure?" which any student knows is code for, "You are wrong. Try again."

I'm sure now that if I'd made any of those choices, Nora would have corrected her reading and moved on, and I would have lost an opportunity for insight and, therefore, teaching. My research mode led me to further curiosity. I was intrigued: How could this girl be such a good reader of one scene and such a poor reader of another? In probing that question, I allowed myself to notice her answers without correcting them.

Ultimately, Nora's answers to my follow-up questions told me *how* she was thinking as she read, not just *what* she was thinking. Nora was lost, yes, but lost in a variety of ways and probably for a number of reasons. It could have been some unfamiliar vocabulary—*clunker*, for example, or *pierces*—or the dialogue that didn't have a tag. It could have been the odd syntax of the sentence, where *jungle cat* modifies *grumble*, or the figurative language—*jungle cat* being descriptive rather than literal. We'll see in Chapter 3 how I used what I noticed to teach from, but first let's look more closely at what frequently gets in the way of our research as we confer with students.

What Gets in the Way

Just as everything in schools seems to conspire against slowing our teaching down, so everything in schools seems to conspire against allowing us to research our students. I believe, however, that if we look squarely at what gets in the way, we will be able to remove some of those barriers.

Teaching as Correcting

In a research conference a text does not have a right or wrong answer; rather, a text has an opening that allows us to notice how our students are comprehending. Accepting this takes an enormous shift in attitude because, frankly, a text often *does* have right and wrong answers. It is *not* Andrew's father speaking on page 66 of *Loser*; it is Donald's. We want to correct that as our students read. We yearn to correct them. The clock is ticking. The state tests are approaching.

But correcting is not teaching. Correcting is small. It's about one word, one sentence, one text. Teaching is bigger. It attempts to take that moment and contextualize it. It attempts to help us help our students see the larger work involved and apply it to other texts. In the case of Nora this larger context might be how to follow dialogue that isn't tagged, but it may also be something bigger, perhaps a strategy or two about how to visualize a scene, or how to keep track of multiple characters or how to deal with confusion. No matter what I ended up teaching Nora, however, I would not have been able to teach her anything had I focused on correcting her. Correcting is not part of my teaching agenda; understanding thinking is.

Teaching the Text

You saw in the conference I highlighted at the beginning of this chapter how trapped I became by inviting the student to summarize the book. First, it ate up all my time. But having students summarize the books they're reading creates more than just time management problems. The bigger problem is one of instruction. I fell into the trap of thinking that teaching consists of teaching the text. It's a common trap and related to the idea of teaching as correcting. How do we know if the student is "getting it" if we haven't read the book? This assumes, of course, that there is an "it" to get and an "it" to teach. This assumes that our job is to teach the "it" rather than the process of thinking that goes into constructing an understanding of an "it."

Lucy Calkins, in *The Art of Teaching Writing*, puts it this way: "If we can keep only one thing in mind . . . it is that we are teaching the writer and not the writing" (Calkins 1994, 228). Translating this into teaching reading, we need to teach the *reader* and not the *reading*, the *thinker* and not the *thoughts*. Getting plot summaries from students, if it teaches anything at all (which I have come to doubt), reaps little information about our students as readers, therefore giving us virtually nothing to teach from.

In my conference with Nora, my lack of knowledge about the book *Loser* actually became an advantage, allowing me to ask genuine questions that led to insight into her thinking. Ironically, I have found that the easiest way to get information about a reader and not the reading is by entering into the text side by side with a student—not the text as a whole, but a small slice of it, a page or a few paragraphs. Rather than asking students to tell me about their book, I ask them to open their book; rather than summarizing, I ask them to read. In this way we can get a little slice of their thinking, a microcosm, and begin to notice what we might possibly teach from there.

Teaching as Evaluation

As I've studied conferring in a variety of schools, I have noticed that many teachers use their conference time to evaluate their students, specifically around the students' reading levels. While I don't entirely disagree with research findings stating that students need to be in "just-right" books in order to read "instructionally" (Allington 2001; Fountas and Pinnell 1996), reading levels have, unfortunately, come to dominate much of the content of our instruction, especially in conferences. Is a child reading at their level? We confer to find out. Have they moved up? We confer to find out.

But too often the only thing we're finding out from those conferences— and the only thing we're delivering to our students as instruction—is a label. Students are being assessed and then told to go to this or that bin to pick out another book—or not. The invitation to see a mind at work has been withdrawn. Even if we happen to be very good at our jobs and know the differences between, say, an N and an O reading level, even if we recognize that a student is most definitely one and not the other, we rarely take the time to unpack that knowledge with the student. We evaluate and trot them off to a new bin. We call the next student, and the first student, happy that he has moved up, has little or no idea how he achieved what he did or what that specifically means.

Teachers and administrators are clearly feeling pressured to evaluate their students and demonstrate evidence of growth. And while much of this work is well intentioned, we need to step back and take a close look at how our preoccupation with levels has influenced instruction. Moving a student up the level ladder is not the same as teaching that student. Levels can be used to help us make visible some of the invisible work of reading, but they can also easily obscure that work. Only when we take the time to get underneath those labels—to make the thinking that students are doing visible to ourselves and our students—can we make appropriate instructional decisions. I'll look more closely at ways to do this in Chapters 4 and 5.

TOOLBOX ➤ HOW TO CONDUCT RESEARCH CONFERENCES

- Begin by explaining to the student what you're about to do and why. Assure him that this is not an evaluation and not about testing, just an attempt to get an idea of what his brain is doing as his eyes take in words.
- Have the student open the book and start reading where she left off. We want fresh thinking, not rehearsed or rehashed thinking.
- Have the student read. I usually like students to read out loud if they are able to do so quietly without disturbing others. Some older students prefer to read to themselves and I might give them a choice. If a student is reading out loud I often give him an opportunity to reread a passage to himself since sometimes when reading out loud students focus more on fluency and less on meaning.
- Follow along.
- Don't have the student read too much. A short section, even a few paragraphs, will do.
- Ask questions that will help you get a feel for what the student may be thinking. Examples:
  - "What's going on here?"
  - "Why do you think the character did (or said) that?"
- Ask follow-up questions that emphasize how the student knew what she knew. Examples:
  - "What made you think that?"
  - "Where did you get that information?"
- If a student emphasizes a particular word as he reads, it might be interesting to ask him why he did that, what he was thinking that signaled him to change his voice there.
- It can sometimes be revealing to ask a student who the pronouns in a passage refer to. Watch how the student problem-solves antecedents and when she answers, always ask as follow-up, "How do you know?"
- If there are passages that include dialogue, particularly unattributed dialogue, you might want to ask the student who is talking and, as always, follow up with, "How do you know?"
- "What feeling do you get from this part?" might be an appropriate question to ask if there's a particular mood or tone or point of tension in a

passage. You could also ask, "What do you think the character might be feeling right now?" The follow-up question "How do you know?" keeps the student firmly in the text and helps you understand what skills he is activating as he reads.

- "Who's telling the story here?" is a question that can get at issues of narration or point of view and character. As always, get in the habit of asking, "How do you know?" or "What clues give you that information?"

- Sometimes it's interesting to ask a student, "What does this part have to do with the rest of the story?" The goal of this question isn't to get a summary of the extended plot of the book so much as it is to see how a student is or isn't integrating the story as she reads.

- If a student is in the middle of a book, I'll often ask if the part she's just read fits into any patterns that have been established so far and, if so, what she makes of that.

- If a student is finishing a book, I might want to elicit some opinions from the student: What does he think the book was trying to accomplish? Did the author succeed? Will this be a book that sticks with him? What did he learn about life from this book? What did he learn about reading from reading this book?

Note: It is most important to adopt a tone of curiosity rather than interrogation as you ask students research questions. Remember, you are not looking for right or wrong answers but for glimpses into how a student is picking up on and putting together textual clues. Getting into the habit of always asking, "How do you know that?" usually keeps students from feeling they are being tested during these research conferences. Researchers are curious, so be curious and don't be afraid to show your students your curiosity.

2

DECIDING SMARTER
Not Teaching—Yet

Answers are closed rooms; questions are open doors that invite us in.
—Nancy Willard

When I was conferring with Nora I was working in her fifth-grade classroom alongside her teacher and a few others from the school. We were studying conferring and crowded around students as they read independently to listen to each other confer. We then pulled away to reflect on what we should teach next. This was the *decide* phase of the conference (Calkins 2001). In a typical classroom setting with a teacher conferring alone, the *decide* phase is often done quickly, even instantaneously, and in isolation. In this context of study, we were privileged to be working collaboratively to weigh the pros and cons of possible next steps we thought would best help each student as we conferred.

Here is the list this group of teachers came up with for Nora:

- building background knowledge or vocabulary that would help her know what a *clunker* is;
- deepening her understanding of figurative language since she didn't seem to understand *jungle cat grumble*;

- rereading to address the fact that she didn't know what was going on;
- visualizing to address the fact that she didn't know what was going on;
- following dialogue that isn't tagged;
- following antecedents to pronouns;
- choosing a book she could be engaged in.

The teachers in the group shared their lists and then looked at me expectantly. I'm sure they thought that I would choose one of these options swiftly and, well, decisively. If Chapter 1 was the place for me to confess what I don't know, this is the place for me to confess that I have a hard time making decisions—a quality that teaching seems to have exacerbated. So many decisions to make and none of them with clear-cut answers: What book to choose for a read-aloud? What to teach first? How to teach it? There are so many variables, so many options, so many valid answers. And while I will admit that some of this agonizing might be idiosyncratic to my personality, I also know that many teachers, like the four who were looking at me in Nora's fifth-grade classroom, often feel the same way: how does one decide what to teach?

The quick answer to this will be to repeat what I said in the first chapter: slow down. Classrooms are not boardrooms and teachers should not necessarily make swift CEO-type decisions, especially regarding reading. This is because so much of the work of reading is invisible. When we make quick decisions, we tend to base those decisions on what is most visible. Look at the possible next steps listed earlier. Each is based on something that was starkly visible as Nora read, and it is no coincidence that each of the items on that list is about correcting something she got wrong. What students get wrong is often the most visible part of reading and therefore the one we most often instruct around.

In case you're thinking this is not necessarily a bad thing, let's consider the old parable of the three stonemasons. When a visitor happened on them, all working in the stone yard, and asked what they were doing, the first stonemason replied, "I'm cutting this stone," the second said, "I'm building a parapet," and the third responded, "I'm building a cathedral." All were doing the same work, of course, but only the third was doing so with vision or purpose. Surely we want our students to be more like that third stonemason than the first—to read with vision and purpose. But when we focus our teaching only on something that will correct a student's reading, we are basically teaching her to focus only on what's directly in front of her, the stone.

If we want our students to read like the third stonemason, our teaching needs vision. We need to see ourselves as building cathedrals rather than merely cutting stone. As we ponder the *decide* phase of our conferences, the question "What can we teach?" actually boxes us in to making quick choices based mainly on what is most visible. Instead, we need to look beyond what students "get" or "don't get" and, therefore, ask ourselves a different question: We need to ask, "What does it mean?" What does it mean, for example, that Nora was following the scene so well in one portion of the text but then got so lost in another? What does it mean that she so easily held on to some details but viewed others with complete confusion? What does it mean that she so automatically ticked off words without seeming to be engaged either in the book or in the process of building meaning?

When we allow ourselves to consider what a reader's actions and behaviors might mean—not just what is visible but what the visible points to—we are more likely to get a glimpse of how the mind and the book are intersecting. This is, of course, the whole point of conferring with students as they read and it is how we, as teachers, can begin to teach with vision, toward that cathedral.

Reading with Vision

Before I move on, let's pause and look at what I mean when I say we need to teach students to read with vision. Metaphors of cathedrals are all well and good, but what does reading with vision really look like?

Let's go back to Nora to examine this question more closely. If I had chosen to teach the first item on our what-to-teach list—her lack of background knowledge about the term *clunker*—she may have improved her comprehension of that one sentence, or at least part of that sentence. But then what? How would that lesson help her with the next sentence or the next book? And even if I had managed to actually teach that lesson in a way that emphasized transfer to other texts and even if Nora took on that transfer, the rationale behind my teaching would still have emphasized the message that texts have an "it" that is to be gotten. And while this might be true on the surface—the word *clunker* does have a specific meaning in the context of that sentence—it does little to convey the active process of reading necessary to truly understand not just the meaning of that one word but why it is capitalized, what it's doing in that scene, how it's been previously introduced in the text, and what its implications are. In other words, there is a much larger context at play, a context that needs to be constructed, one word at a time, a context that allows a reader not only to comprehend the literal word on the page but also to understand its larger significance in the narrative.

If as teachers we focus only on what is most visible in a reading conference, we are paying attention only to the smallest unit of comprehension and not acknowledging the process of reading that leads to deeper comprehension and understanding. Even in this age of testing, where answers matter, teachers need to see that those answers come out of a complex interaction between the text and the reader. As Louise Rosenblatt classically put it, "A story or poem or play is merely inkspots on paper until a reader transforms them into a set of meaningful symbols" (2005, 62). Paying attention to and teaching into that process of transforming inkspots into meaning is, ultimately, our job as teachers of reading.

Reading with Agency

Constructing meaning is an active, ongoing process. And what is most needed to sustain such a process is a sense of what Peter Johnston calls "agency." Agency, he writes, is a basic understanding that "the environment is responsive to our actions" (2004, 29). In other words, when we act there are consequences, and when we encounter problems we can act strategically to solve those problems and attain goals. Despite being a character in a fable, the stonemason who was aware of the cathedral he was working on while cutting a piece of stone was exhibiting agency. He was exerting power over his life in a way that his coworkers were not simply because he attached his actions to something that had a consequence and that resulted in meaning.

Nora did not appear to be reading with a sense of agency. She was not reading for meaning, that much was clear, but more important, she did not seem to sense that in order to read for meaning she needed to be an active participant in that process. She was obeying orders, reading words on a page but constructing nothing.

Unfortunately, I see such behaviors more and more among students, perhaps reflections of the teaching they're receiving, whether it is an early childhood program that emphasizes mechanics over meaning and purpose (Gallas 1994) or a high school curriculum that inadvertently shows reading "as something that competent students or adults do in a single pass, in one effortless draft, without struggle and without frustration" (Blau 2003, 31).

The Common Core State Standards (CCSS) and much of the accompanying assessments and support materials seem to be taking this same stance, emphasizing the text over the way in which meaning is negotiated. Teachers, for example, are being urged to formulate "text-dependent questions" that point to particular clues in the text that will supposedly unlock and reveal meaning. Such instruction sends specific messages about what it means to read, messages that privilege the text and the teacher's process of making meaning over the student's. Do we really think our students are blank slates waiting to receive meaning, despite decades of research that has proved otherwise (Wells 2009)? Or do we believe, as Gordon Wells puts it, that "teaching is essentially a matter of facilitating learning . . . where the aim must be the *collaborative* construction of meaning" (2009, 113). If we believe the latter, we have to agree that students need to be agents in the reading process and we, as teachers, need to situate them to be active constructors of meaning.

Reading with a Flexible Mindset

We cannot emphasize student agency if we think about thinking as fixed. Peter Johnston explores this concept in *Opening Minds* (2012), building on the work of psychologist Carol Dweck (2006). Her research describes people with two different mindsets: one she calls fixed, which emphasizes a view of oneself as predetermined or static, and one she calls growth, which views the self as dynamic and cultivated through effort. Dweck's research is fascinating, and Johnston's application of her concepts to the language of teaching is essential reading. It's important for teachers to apply the idea of fixed and flexible mindsets to texts as well as people. If we view texts as having a fixed meaning, we will view the thinking in that text as fixed; if we view texts as having meaning that is dynamically realized, or constructed through an active process, we will view the thinking in that text as flexible.

In case this sounds too theoretical, think about a time you saw a movie and talked with someone about it afterward. You probably left the theater with ideas and responses to the film, then talked with a friend about it and realized your ideas were shifting and growing. You considered things you hadn't noticed before and noticed other things in a new light. Those of us who are readers certainly know this to be true with books. Meaning making is an active process requiring a flexible mindset.

And while many teachers have some structures in place that accommodate this understanding—discussion time for read-aloud texts or book clubs or literature circles, where students meet in small groups to talk about one book (Daniels 2002)—when it comes to independent reading, we often unwittingly undermine our students' flexible thinking. Focusing our conferences on levels, for example, sends messages to students that there is an "it" to get in a text and those who get it climb the level ladder swiftly while others don't. Likewise, when we focus our next instructional steps on what students get or don't get in a text, we are emphasizing knowledge over learning, product over process.

So how do we tweak our teaching to convey messages about reading and thinking that emphasize flexible and dynamic thinking over fixed and static knowledge? How do we teach with vision so our students can read with vision?

Teaching with Vision: Noticing the How Not Just the What

The first thing we can do is pay attention not just to what our students know but how they know what they know. As Peter Johnston puts it, "The strongest thread in the warp of the dynamic-learning fabric is attention to processes, particularly causal processes" (2012, 31). In conferring, this can be deceptively simple to do: In addition to paying attention to what a student is comprehending, we can ask follow-up questions such as, "How do you know that?" or "Where did you get that information?" or "What did you read that gave you that idea?" I could ask a child reading *Frog and Toad Are Friends* by Arnold Lobel (1970), for example, what's going on in the passage given here:

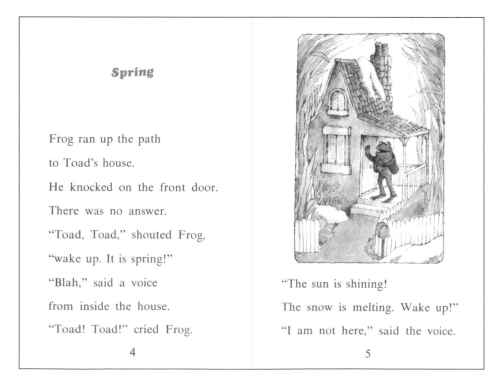

Spring

Frog ran up the path
to Toad's house.
He knocked on the front door.
There was no answer.
"Toad, Toad," shouted Frog,
"wake up. It is spring!"
"Blah," said a voice
from inside the house.
"Toad! Toad!" cried Frog.

4

"The sun is shining!
The snow is melting. Wake up!"
"I am not here," said the voice.

5

Let's say that child tells me this: "Frog is going over to Toad's house and Toad doesn't want to come outside." Instead of moving on because I'm satisfied that the child is comprehending the page, I could ask, "How do you know Toad doesn't want to come outside?" The child would then presumably point to any number of textual clues that gave her that information: the picture; the fact that Frog knocked on the front door and there was no answer; the fact that a voice from inside the house says, *"Blah."*

Another child might say something like this: "Frog is excited to play with Toad." Again, if I ask a how-do-you-know question, such as, "How do you know Frog is excited?" the child might point to the picture, to the words *shouted* or *cried*, to the phrase *It is spring!*, or to the fact that Frog was running. He might point to all those clues or he might point to only one—a testament to the fact that meaning is a dynamic process consisting of putting together many clues in many different ways.

Noticing how students accomplish something rather than simply focusing on the accomplishment itself provides teachers with many opportunities to notice process and effort over product and ability. In my conference with Nora, for example, when I moved beyond the what to the how by asking her how she knew that Donald was wearing his father's helmet to help him deliver mail, her reply—that the information was stated on a previous page—helped me glimpse what she was doing as a reader, her process. I could see that she was holding on to information from one page to another. On the face of it, this may seem obvious—of course she was holding on to information from one page to another, that's what readers do—but as we can see from her confusion about the other details (*his father's voice, the jungle cat grumble,* and *Clunker Four*), this is not always such simple work, nor so consistently done. Nora was doing something with some details and doing nothing with others. She connected the detail of the helmet to another section of the text, but did not do that—or even seem to consider doing that—with the details of *his father's voice* or *the jungle cat grumble* or *Clunker Four*. Every detail does something in a text; and every reader, in turn, needs to do something with those details—which is, of course, why we need to see what students are *doing*, not just what they are *knowing*.

What enabled me to notice this with Nora was my experience as a reader. I know how texts work and what my brain has to do as a result. I know, in this example, that authors of narrative texts plant details and return to them, developing and growing them into significance through the course of the story. I know, therefore, that I have to hold on to those details, sometimes only for a paragraph or two but sometimes for pages, through chapters, until the very end of a book, in order to understand their part in the narrative. When I read the words *Clunker Four* over Nora's shoulder, I knew that there must have been a previous reference to this odd phrase even though I hadn't read the book. I knew that Jerry Spinelli was most likely not introducing his readers to this thing, whatever it might be, for the first time on this page in this manner. The way it was written signaled to me that it had been introduced earlier.

My challenge as Nora's teacher was that although I knew that *Clunker Four* was not just a detail sitting there, inert, I also knew that if I emphasized this as something I was getting and Nora was not, I would be emphasizing the text over the thinking about the text, the what over the how, the fixed-frame knowledge over the dynamic-learning frame.

So how could I teach her? How could I help her?

Teaching Readers to Be Problem Solvers

The predicament we often face as teachers is that we want to teach students to get what we think should be gotten from the page. I wanted and expected Nora to know who was saying, *"No peeking,"* and to know what *Clunker Four* was because that's what getting the text involved. When we confer with students who don't get it, like Nora, we often perform all sorts of verbal twists and turns in order to teach them to see what they're not getting. Think about what we really mean when we say things like, "Are you sure?" or "Let's look at that word again." But all those moves—no matter how artfully or considerately made—are doing one thing: situating *us* as the problem solvers in a text. We are zeroing in on aspects of comprehension that we deem to be lacking, stopping students when they make mistakes, pointing out their errors, narrowing our vision to what they don't get, and then proceeding to teach them how they could or should get it.

In a traditional conference with Nora, for example, I could have taught one thing on the list that the study-group teachers made, a list that amounts to all the things she wasn't getting—her vocabulary and background knowledge, her understanding of figurative language, her book choices. But by doing that I would have been the one pointing out when and where she wasn't comprehending and what she would need to do to correct that. Nora, in turn, could have taken that teaching and done any number of things with it. Of course I like to think that she'd skip away, internalizing whatever I delivered. But the truth is, she might just as easily have discarded what I taught or pretended to understand. She could have listened politely and then forgotten what I had said or have no idea how to put what I taught into place in another text. The point is that no matter what her response, I would have been the problem solver in the situation, not Nora, and my teaching would have done nothing to shift that capacity from my domain to hers.

If we agree that reading is a "constructive, problem-solving" process, "which increases in power and flexibility the more it is practiced" (Clay 1991, 2, 6), then teachers cannot be the problem solvers for students. Instead, we need to situate students to be problem solvers.

This is not always easy. Let's look at Nora. She seemed not to be problem-solving at all. In fact, her lack of comprehension seemed to have no significance to her. She read the words, doing her job much as the first stonemason did his job, simply cutting the stone with no larger purpose in sight. When I stopped her at that odd *Clunker Four* sentence, she *did* seem to be aware that she wasn't comprehending but registered that only as a minor blip, perhaps because she saw the sentence as having little or no bearing on the general plot of the book.

If Nora had been reading as a problem solver, her lack of comprehension about that sentence would have ground her process to a halt. It would have appeared as a problem, a problem she would have to solve—if she had been taught she had the agency to do so. Perhaps she would have noticed that she was unaware of who was speaking the words *"No peeking,"* or couldn't quite determine in what tone they were being delivered. Perhaps she would have recognized that she didn't understand what *jungle cat grumble* meant and what it had to do with this other confusing thing, *Clunker Four*. Perhaps she would have asked herself what this odd sentence had to do with what had come before—the scene about Donald delivering mail with his father, and also the preceding scenes. Perhaps she would be considering how this detail might be clarified as she continued to read, in which case she would have understood that she wasn't supposed to know—at least not yet—what *Clunker Four* or the *jungle cat grumble* were. Perhaps she would have wondered how this odd sentence contributed to a larger understanding of these characters, their relationships and circumstances, the problems or issues they might be facing, and how they are attempting to solve or reconcile themselves with what is happening to them—in other words, why the author chose to place this detail here, and what purpose it might serve to the overall narrative.

A different kind of student might have recognized any of these things, but not Nora. She was doing none of those things. So now what?

Setting Texts Up as Problems to Be Solved

One of the simplest ways to set students up as problem solvers is to set texts up as problems to be solved. By this I don't mean the kind of problem that might be equated with a thankless task or chore (think Dante's *Inferno* for summer reading), but rather a roll-up-your-sleeves-and-puzzle-it-out kind of problem. Texts are tricky: they aren't always written in a straightforward manner; they don't come right out and state information. Rather, as Vicki Vinton and I explored in *What Readers Really Do*, they "show" in order to "tell" (Barnhouse and Vinton 2012). In narrative texts, for example, writers use character, action, dialogue, description, imagery, and details to convey both what is literally happening in the story as well as ideas and themes they are exploring. In nonfiction texts, writers also convey information and ideas in indirect ways—through carefully chosen examples or anecdotes, repeated words or ideas, the juxtaposition of images, or the accumulation of related facts, to name a few. Texts, no matter what their level, have explicit or "told" as well as implicit or "shown" layers, a concept explored further in Chapter 4.

Even a seemingly simple text is designed to reveal information through the reading experience or process—in other words, in transaction with the reader. Let's look again at the first page of *Frog and Toad Are Friends* to see how this works:

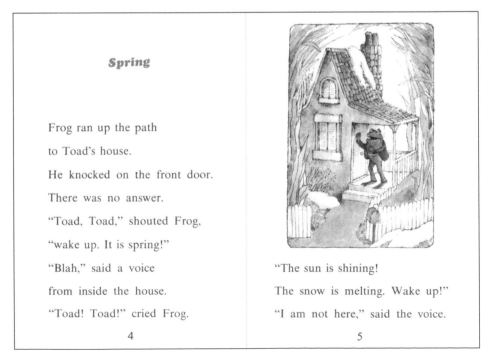

Spring

Frog ran up the path
to Toad's house.
He knocked on the front door.
There was no answer.
"Toad, Toad," shouted Frog,
"wake up. It is spring!"
"Blah," said a voice
from inside the house.
"Toad! Toad!" cried Frog.

4

"The sun is shining!
The snow is melting. Wake up!"
"I am not here," said the voice.

5

This text explicitly tells us a few things—what Frog is doing (running) and where he is going (up the path to Toad's house). But it doesn't tell us why he is running up the path, nor what he might be thinking or how he might be feeling. And because one person's explicit is another's implicit, we can imagine that if you were new to pronouns and didn't know how they worked in the English language, it also might not be apparent who the *He* is who is knocking on the door. You could use the picture, of course, but even that is a clue and not a directly stated piece of information. It requires that a reader actively make a connection between the sentence and the picture. Likewise, the text does not explicitly state who is saying, *"Blah,"* though we are given direct information that it is *a voice* and that the voice is coming from *inside the house*.

The reader of *Frog and Toad*, therefore, has to actively connect one sentence to another: the *he* in the second sentence needs to be connected to *Frog* in the first; the voice in the fifth sentence needs to be connected with *Toad* in the fourth; the picture needs to be connected to the words.

This provides teachers with a perfect opportunity to pose texts as problems to be solved. If, in a conference with a student reading this page, for example, we determine that the student is not considering how Frog might be feeling or not thinking about who could be saying, *"Blah,"* we pose that as a problem. We could say, as I said with Nora, that this is a tricky text. We can say something like, "Hmm. This text doesn't say how Frog is feeling. How could we figure that out?" (See Chapter 3 for an actual conference with a student reading these pages.)

Recognizing with students that texts are problems to be solved helps us avoid portraying students as problem readers. Asking a how-can-we-figure-out question is the pedagogical opposite of pointing out to students what they did not get. The latter might sound something like this: "Are you sure?" or "Look again at that" or "This book isn't your level." Those statements send messages that frame the reader as having problems. How-can-we-figure-out questions frame texts as having problems.

In other texts and other reading experiences, such as in read-aloud, we might support this work by saying, "How can we figure out something when it's not stated?" Depending on the age of your students and the type of books they're reading, that something might be as basic as who is talking or what the character's name is or as abstract as what we call *theme* or *main idea* (Chapters 5 and 6 provide examples of this teaching). Or, depending on the genre or the text we're in or even the page or the paragraph, a reader might need to figure out where a character is or why this paragraph (or sidebar or sentence or anecdote or description) is here or what one part has to do with another or why the author chose this image or ending or why this angle on this topic.

In a seventh-grade class reading *Wonder* by R. J. Palacio, for example, students noticed that the author was switching points of view as the story unfolded. Initially they thought of this simply as a "craft" move, something fancy the author dreamed up in order to "make the book more interesting" for the reader. But as they continued reading, doing the work of interpretation by noticing patterns and asking and answering why questions around those patterns (Barnhouse and Vinton 2012), they came up with rich and varied ideas about what this move allowed the author to convey to her audience and how it did or did not support her themes and messages.

They did the figuring out work because the teacher expected them to do so. (The question, "Why is the author switching points of view?" remained on a class chart for several weeks as they made their way through the book.) They also did the figuring out work because the book expected them to do so. The author's reasons for using different points of view are, of course, not explained or explicitly revealed in the narrative and therefore provided an opportunity for these students to problem-solve. This high-level thinking task consisted simply of allowing students to notice—in this case the switching points of view—and to do something with what they noticed—to grapple with questions that it sparked. This is no small task in an era of highly prescribed instruction, for it requires that the students, rather than the teacher, take on the role of noticing and questioning, but it's one that pays off immensely for students.

Virtually all the work that readers do in texts—whether to comprehend what is literally on the page or to interpret an author's move—can be phrased as a problem to be solved. Creating these opportunities involves only opening a book and stepping aside, allowing students to listen to texts. Doing so actively engages students, which helps them build agency and flexible mindsets as they read. This also helps them build their schemas of how texts work (see Chapter 4), which in turn helps them learn more about reading every time they read (Clay 1991, 288).

Learning from Errors

Situating our students to be problem solvers requires that we remain patient as they make their way through texts: every student will not necessarily make the exact same inference at the exact time and from the exact same clues that we do (Barnhouse and Vinton 2012). We have to trust, however, that the process will pay off. If we short-circuit our students' thinking, they will fail to learn that reading is an intellectual enterprise. This leads, inevitably, to the issue of errors. If we are to allow students to be problem solvers, we have to understand that they will make errors. Many educators recognize that errors are at the heart of learning (Wells 2009). Jason Moser, a psychologist at Michigan State University, in attempting to study how some people learn faster than others, found that people who improved their performance on an assigned task were the ones who paid closer attention to their errors. No surprise that these same people were identified as having growth mindsets rather than fixed mindsets (Moser et al. 2011).

And yet most schools in the United States operate within a system that treats errors as indicators of a fixed trait rather than an opportunity for growth. "She's a '2,'" says a teacher, referring to a student's standardized test score—and no wonder, since that score, in turn, will become part of the teacher's performance assessment, another fixed-frame indicator. Since data has taken a front seat to instruction, product has eclipsed process. But meaning making is not a simple, linear act; it is a complex process involving the accumulations of multiple cues that readers constantly check and cross-check. The product cannot be separated from its process. We therefore need instruction that emphasizes errors as natural by-products of the process of reading. Sheridan Blau, in *The Literature Workshop*, seeks to reframe errors—not as mistakes but as a source of confusion that "often represents an advanced state of understanding" (2003, 21). Teachers, therefore, should not "anticipate and prevent . . . confusion, but . . . welcome and even foster among readers the experience of confusion" (21).

The rewards of struggling through confusion are apparent to anyone who has experienced an enlightened "Oh" after they've worked through trying to understand something. I saw the power of "Oh" in a first-grade class I was working with recently. Two students, Wyatt and Julia, were reading the book *Silly Milly* together. *Silly Milly* is structured like a riddle. It tells the reader things that Milly likes and things that Milly doesn't like, leaving the reader to guess why: *She likes green. She does not like red. She likes butter. She does not like bread. She likes seeds. She does not like flowers* (Lewison 2010).

On the next page—*She likes umbrellas. She does not like showers.*—Wyatt turned to Julia and said, "I don't get why she says this."

"She only likes things with double letters," replied Julia, factually. "Let me show you." She then pointed to the word *umbrella* and turned back a page to point to the word *seeds*.

"Oh," said Wyatt, but it was a lukewarm response. He pressed on, "But why does she only like things with double letters?"

Julia shrugged and turned the page to keep reading but Wyatt stopped her. "I actually think I know why! Her name is double letters: *Silly* and *Milly*."

"Oh!" said Julia, full of surprise and recognition. "Yeah." She then proceeded to look back at each of the pages she'd already read, looking more closely at the illustrations, which depicted items with double-letter words ("Jelly," Julia said, pointing to the picture. "Yellow." "Puppy."). Wyatt turned away from the book at that point and looked at the classroom walls, which were full of labels and student writing. "Look," he said, walking over to point to where the word *book* appeared. "Double-letter word. And here [he pointed to the word *buddy*]. Double-letter word."

As the class finished up their work, Wyatt was still reading the walls of the classroom, naming to whomever was within listening distance all the double-letter words he was now noticing. Perhaps he identified with *Silly Milly*, since his own name had a double letter, but looking at Julia buried in the book and Wyatt roaming the room, I saw two students exhilarated at working through confusion together to arrive at deeper understanding and engagement.

As students grapple with errors and confusion, we can do one of two things. We can be "item-oriented," as Marie Clay calls it, stepping in to correct the error or "direct the pupil," or we can be "strategy-oriented," helping the child become an independent problem solver (Clay 1991, 300). Helping our students become independent problem solvers means we can watch as they problem-solve and then name the thinking processes we notice. To Wyatt and Julia, I ended up saying, "Did you see how you asked a 'why' question, which you then answered together? That helped you notice something you hadn't noticed before!"

As Peter Johnston reminds us, "Process information removes the 'genius' from performance and replaces it with both a dynamic-learning frame and the strategic knowledge of how the success was accomplished" (Johnston 2012, 31). I'll add to that by saying that process information also removes the "dummy" from errors and replaces it with both a dynamic-learning frame and the strategic knowledge of how the problem was solved.

Building Identities as Thinkers and Learners

Emphasizing what our students do in order to solve the problems that texts pose is important not just for reading; it's also vital as we help students build identities as thinkers and learners. I think about this often when I'm in classrooms and talk casually with students about their reading. "Tell me about some of your favorite books," I often ask and some of their replies are heart-breaking: "I'm a J," a second grader once told me; or "I read with Mrs. _____ [the pull-out teacher]"; or, perhaps the worst and also the most common, a shrug.

As I listen to students like these, I think first of the diet that we're subjecting them to: workbooks or computer programs with specifically written texts or exercises positioned to teach skills in isolation; textbooks with excerpts from texts; guided reading sets. I then think of how that diet has become a kind of mirror we're holding up to these students. They are constructing their identities based on what we're showing them. I'm reminded of what the Nigerian author Chimamanda Adichie calls the dangers of a single story. She describes how single stories—whether about a person or a group of people—lead to misunderstandings and close-mindedness. She gives as examples stories about poor Africans that have become the predominant image that non-Africans have of Africans. "The single story creates stereotypes," she says, "and the problem with stereotypes is not that they are untrue, but that they are incomplete. They make one story become the only story" (Adichie 2009).

When there's only one story, and it's told over and over, people become those stories.

How often in our conferences are we telling a single story to our students merely because we are continually stepping in to be the problem solvers? From our stance, they are getting messages about their reading abilities, about their identities as readers and learners, and about the act of reading itself.

So before we decide what we need to teach, we need to decide what messages we want to send to students through our conferences: Will we tell a single story, a story that holds out comprehension as an "it" that a student gets or doesn't, that puts us in the position of knowing and the student in the position of not knowing? Or will we tell stories that highlight how students know what they know, showing them the dynamic, flexible thinking and problem solving that is the essence of reading?

 TOOLBOX **HOW TO SITUATE OUR STUDENTS TO BECOME PROBLEM SOLVERS**

- First, think about yourself as a reader. Read a page of a book and think about what you know and how you know it. Use the following two-column chart to keep track of your thinking (Figure 2.1 and Appendix 1; see also Chapter 5).

Figure 2.1 A chart to help you think about how you know what you know in a text, filled in with *Frog and Toad Are Friends*

What I Know (from the text)	How I Know It
Frog is running	Stated
Frog is going to Toad's house	Stated
Frog is excited	Picture + *shouted* and *cried* + *"It is spring!"* + *"The sun is shining!"*

○ In the opening of *Frog and Toad*, for example, what is explicitly told and what is implicitly revealed? What is given to you? What do you have to figure out? What clues are you using to help you do that figuring-out work?

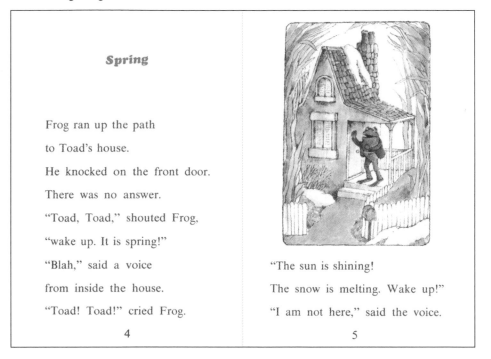

Spring

Frog ran up the path

to Toad's house.

He knocked on the front door.

There was no answer.

"Toad, Toad," shouted Frog,

"wake up. It is spring!"

"Blah," said a voice

from inside the house.

"Toad! Toad!" cried Frog.

4

"The sun is shining!

The snow is melting. Wake up!"

"I am not here," said the voice.

5

- Now think about your students. Think about what is explicit and what might be implicit for them in a text.
  ○ Find out *what* they are comprehending (by asking "What's going on here?").
  ○ Find out *how* they are comprehending (by asking "How do you know?" or "What made you think that?").
- Hold off on evaluation.
  ○ Instead of saying, "You're right" or "Are you sure?" continue to ask how-do-you-know or what-made-you-think-that questions.
- Situate the text as a problem to be solved.
  ○ Do this by acknowledging, "This text is tricky," or "This text doesn't come right out and say . . ."
  ○ Ask how-can-you-figure-out questions
    + about basic information in texts, such as what a character's name is or who is talking; and
    + about big-thinking work, such as character motivation, main idea, or theme.

- ○ Ask "why" questions and encourage students to do the same
  - + about craft or style moves; and
  - + about characters and why they're doing what they're doing.
- Encourage students to notice and allow them to do something with what they notice.
  - ○ Ask, "What do you notice?" and "What does that make you think?"
- Encourage students to look closely at places where they were confused, not because they might have gotten it wrong but because that means they've come to a "tricky" part that needs to be solved.
  - ○ Listen so you can try to notice and name the processes you see them using to problem-solve.
- Recognize the payoff that results from problem solving. Intellectual work is satisfying.
- Keep your mouth shut. Students have to trust that you aren't just temporarily giving them a get-out-of-jail-free card. They will say to you, "What's the answer?" but you will not answer. Students are players in this game, not audience members; it is their meaning to construct.

TEACHING SMARTER
Noticing and Naming

The whole purpose of education is to turn mirrors into windows.
—Sydney J. Harris

I was struggling through a yoga class once and the teacher walked around the room, adjusting everyone's poses, making comments and suggestions. When she got to me, attempting a pose where my heels were supposed to be flat on the floor but were nowhere near, she said, "I love the way your heels are yearning toward the floor." I had to laugh. That certainly was one way of looking at it. But during class the following week, I found myself "yearning" my heels a little more toward the floor, and in the weeks following I became more conscious of yearning other parts of myself into other poses. In short, I began to view myself not in hopeless contrast to the amazing double-jointed dancers who populated the class, but as someone engaged in a process—and thereby more likely to eventually meet the goal of getting my heels on the floor.

My yoga teacher's words functioned as a mirror for me that day, helping me focus on what I was doing rather than on how far I needed to go. If she had said something along the lines of, "Try to get your heels closer to the floor," no matter how supportive her tone or her intention, it would have conveyed that my heels were too far off the ground. In response, I probably would have thought, "Yeah, right." But because she described something I was already doing, I felt I could keep doing that, which, in turn, helped me do it better and begin to apply it to other parts of my practice.

Noticing and Naming

In a conference setting, students learn about what they are doing from what we say to them. Our conferences are little mirrors for our students. We therefore have to look very carefully at what our words are teaching them. Are we teaching them that they can or that they can't? Are we teaching them that they have agency or not? My yoga teacher's language mattered. How she said what she said was, in and of itself, a form of teaching. Don Graves reminds us that smart teaching is not about being the "chief informant"—telling "students about what they ought to know"—but rather helping "children to teach us about what they know." One of the best ways to do this, he writes, is to "confirm that what they have already done is accurate" (1994, 17, 18). Peter Johnston makes a similar point in *Choice Words*, describing this form of teaching as "noticing and naming" (2004, 13).

Before I explore this further, let me clarify something about the term *naming* that has come up as I've worked with teachers on this: naming does not necessarily mean putting an academic term to something a student is doing, such as "You're inferring," or "That's a symbol." Nor does naming mean introducing the student to the world of educator jargon, such as "You're now a level P," or "I'm noticing you're using all three cueing systems to figure out that word." Rather, naming in this context is more of a description or explanation of what a student is doing and how they know what they know, in other words the process by which they understand something. If we have taken the opportunity in our reading conferences to notice smarter, as described in Chapter 2, we can name what we notice, which will help us teach smarter.

Let's look at Nora again, whom I introduced in Chapter 1, to illuminate what this looks like. We're picking up the conference where we left off, with Nora reading page 66 of *Loser* by Jerry Spinelli. Here is the portion of the text that we have been talking about:

> *The first house has a slot. Donald slips a letter through. He listens for it to land but he cannot hear it. The slot is eye-high. Quietly, with his finger, he pushes in the swinging brass flap. He takes off his helmet and*

scrunches his eyeball to the slot and strains to see the letter on the floor. All he can make out is a green carpet. He looks around some more, hoping to spot something interesting, but all he sees is an ordinary living room with furniture and a picture on the wall of four basset hounds playing cards.

"No peeking!"

His father's voice pierces the jungle cat grumble of Clunker Four, prowling slowly along in the street. Donald lets the brass flapper swing down. He replaces his helmet and goes back to work. (Spinelli 2002, 66)

Nora is seemingly completely lost and here is how I'm continuing the conference. You can see that I am still in the *research* mode, trying to determine what Nora is doing:

DB: When it says *His father's voice*, do we know whose father the narrator is referring to?

Nora: Donald's?

DB: OK, how do you know that?

Nora: Andrew's?

DB: Oh, you're changing your mind. How come? What information in the text is telling you it could be Andrew's father's voice—or maybe Donald's?

Nora: [Silent.]

DB: OK. So you're not sure whether *his voice* is Andrew's or Donald's father. Pronouns are tricky. Sometimes it's easy to lose track of who they're referring to.

But you know what? I saw you doing similar work up here, with the helmet. That part didn't make sense to me—why a mail carrier would be wearing a helmet—but you knew because you remembered information you'd gotten from earlier in the chapter. You went right back to the place in the text and pointed to the sentence that helped you know this was a mail carrier's helmet.

I'm wondering if that kind of thinking could help you here—if there's information earlier in the text that might explain some of the things that are confusing about this sentence, like whose voice this is, or even what *the jungle cat* is referring to or what the *Clunker Four* is.

Nora: [Nods.]

DB: If you went back a little on this page, or maybe the previous page, maybe even an earlier chapter, you might be able to figure out some of the things that are confusing here. Do you want to try with me?

Nora: OK.

DB: So let's try the first question you have, which is whether this voice is Andrew's dad or Donald's dad. Why don't you look back on this page and see if you can get an answer to that question.

Nora [after rereading silently]: It's Donald's.

DB: Wow! You sound sure of yourself this time. How do you know?

Nora: It says *he* everywhere on this page. And it says *Donald* up here. [Points to *Donald slips a letter through.*] So *his* must be Donald too.

Naming What Students Are Doing to Solve Problems

In this section of the conference, I tried to name something Nora had done as a reader, and done successfully. What I saw her do was hold on to a detail—the helmet—that was provided on one page in order to make sense of its reference on another page. Now she hadn't done this consciously; she was just doing it. She didn't need to be aware of her thinking because she had done it competently. As Marie Clay reminds us, readers don't usually need to be conscious of how they know what they know because "attention is paid to the messages rather than to the work done to get to the message" (Clay 2001, 127). But since my role in this conference was to help Nora see what she had done accurately, I needed her to see something she hadn't seen—not something she was missing in the text but something she hadn't been aware of because she had done it well.

It's important to note that confirming what a student has already done successfully is more than simply offering a compliment. Compliments are considered to be important components of conferences (Calkins 2001; Collins 2004), but I didn't just compliment Nora about something she was doing well and then move on to something she needed to do. Instead, I tried to use what she was doing well to build my teaching point. Many compliments in conferences contain an implicit "but" message, as in, "You did a great job there, but over here you need a little more work." Building a teaching point from a compliment means reframing a "but" to an "and" message, as in, "You did a great job there and now you can do the same here."

Even more effective are "because" messages. These involve describing to the student *how* they accomplished that "great job." A "because" message will sound something like this: "You did a great job there *because* you did such-and-such and now you can do that same such-and-such here." This is naming how a student solved a problem.

Let's pick back up in the conference with Nora to see how I tried to name for her how she problem-solved. When Nora figured out that *His father's voice* was referring to Donald's father, here is how I responded:

DB: Do you see what you did? Parts of this sentence were confusing so you went back to find the signal in the text, the clue, that helped clear up the confusion.

　Maybe the same type of thinking can help with the other parts of the sentence that are confusing—the *jungle cat* and *Clunker Four*. We don't know what that sentence is about—is this a cat? Is this a place? We're not sure.

　What you did with the helmet and the pronoun with *his father's voice* you can do with other things that might at first seem confusing or random.

　You know now that authors don't usually throw random things into the middle of the story. They introduce things on one page and come back to those things in later paragraphs or pages, like the helmet. So maybe the author has already given some information about *Clunker Four* or *the jungle cat grumble* and what you need to do is stop and flip back a bit to find those parts so this part can make sense.

As I'm talking with Nora, I'm jotting notes, diagrams really, trying to make the thinking I'm describing more visual. I do this a lot in conferences, partially because it helps me as I'm talking with students and partially because it seems to help students see the thinking they did. With Nora I wrote the words that didn't make sense to her in a column labeled *Huh?* I included *helmet*, which didn't make sense to me. I then wrote down the clues she used that helped her make sense of those words and labeled that column *Oh!* (Figure 3.1 and Appendix 2). I inserted a two-way arrow between the columns to convey the back-and-forth work that a reader does, moving from confusion to clarity by making within-text connections between pages (Barnhouse and Vinton 2012).

　I leave Nora with my notes, those two unanswered *Huh?*s lingering on the page. Will she go back and search for clues that will help her reach an *Oh!* understanding? A part of me is uneasy. I haven't read the book. I'm betting the entire conference on my hunch that Jerry Spinelli didn't just throw in these details for the first time on page 66. But even if I'm wrong, even if these might be the kinds of details that are planted here for the first time and then explained later in the text—in the next paragraph or page or subsequent chapters—I know that the same kind of thinking will help Nora as she

Figure 3.1
A diagram of the thinking Nora was doing, moving from confusion to clarity by connecting pages

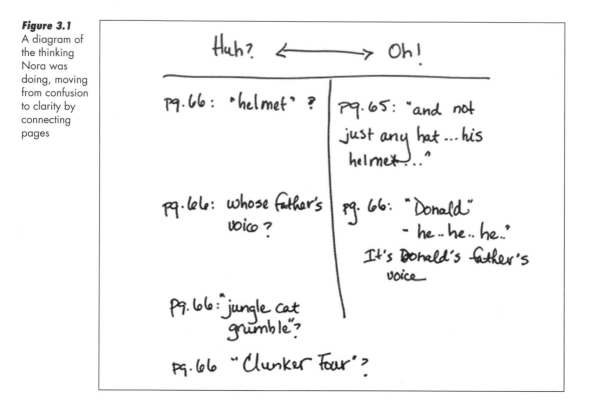

reads forward. I know that my noticing and naming have confirmed that her problem-solving process was accurate (Graves 1994). If this is the only teaching I do in this conference, surely that's enough.

Naming How Texts Work

But it wasn't the only teaching I did. In addition to noticing and naming Nora's thinking, I tried to notice and name why she had to do this kind of thinking to begin with. In other words, I noticed and named something about how texts work. I tried to do this toward the end of the conference when I said:

DB: You know now that authors don't usually throw random things into the middle of the story. They introduce things on one page and come back to those things in later paragraphs or pages, like the helmet.

In pointing this out, I was trying to attach her growing awareness about how details work in one text to a larger schema that will help her in all of her reading. This fleshes out the "because" part of the because messages we want to provide for students. The bones of this teaching sound something like this: "You did a great job there BECAUSE you did such-and-such AND BECAUSE that's the way texts work, so now you know to do the same thing in other texts."

Noticing and naming how texts work—and doing so alongside students—builds their understanding that texts are problems to be solved and allows them to see how practicing something—in this case reading—helps them build an understanding of how that thing works—in this case books. This in turn helps them get better at doing that something.

This is very much like the role of practice in learning a sport. The practice doesn't just increase our ability by building the muscles we use; it also increases our understanding of how that sport works. I saw this clearly when my older daughter was first learning how to play soccer at the age of six or seven. Every kid on her team spent the game huddled in a mass trying to make contact with the ball. The coach would remind the players over and over to spread out. It was his mantra. "I want to work on spreading out," he would instruct before practices, and during games he would yell continually from the sidelines, "Spread out!" But the players only began to spread out as he helped them notice, through lots of practice and game time, that having players in various positions across the field actually helped them score more than when they simply ran after the ball together. The coach didn't just continue to nag the players to spread out, but specified at each opportunity how that strategy had helped them literally accomplish their goals. In this way, the team developed an understanding of how the game worked—it wasn't simply about kicking the ball between goal posts—and the strategy the coach was trying to instill in them began to make sense because its value had become apparent.

Noticing and naming how texts work as we simultaneously notice and name how students are thinking in those texts helps us strengthen the connection between teaching our students strategies and teaching them to be strategic (Johnston 2004). Think about how my conference with Nora could have gone: Because I noticed that she was missing details that she would presumably get if she reread, I could have told her to do just that, to reread. That's a vital strategy and one I completely believe in. But simply telling her to reread does not mean she's going to do it. In fact, rereading is one of those strategies that Vicki Vinton and I have dubbed a pick-up-your-socks strategy (Barnhouse and Vinton 2012), since teachers are constantly telling students to do it and students are constantly ignoring us. Nor does telling Nora to reread mean she's going to reread strategically. In other words, telling her to

Figure 3.2 A Book/Brain chart filled in from a noticing and naming conference with Nora

How Texts Work (Book)	⟷	How Thinking Works (Brain)
Details are sometimes planted on one page and then referred to later		We hold on to details from one page to another We think back as we read forward We reread if a detail doesn't make sense

do something does not guarantee she'll know when to do it or what it helps her accomplish. But framing the strategy in a conference where I am consciously attaching it to a larger understanding about how texts work helps me highlight why this strategy is necessary—and what the payoff can be.

I like to visualize the thinking readers do about how texts work as a two-column chart. On one side is an ongoing list of what a reader is learning about how books work, on the other is a list of the thinking the reader is doing. In between is one of my favorite symbols, a double arrow, because it conveys fluid thinking rather than a linear cause and effect. Sometimes readers do specific thinking and therefore become aware of how texts work (as was the case with Nora); and sometimes readers are aware of how texts work and therefore do specific thinking. As I worked with one group of teachers on creating these charts with their students, they began to refer to them as Book/Brain charts. The term stuck. Figure 3.2 is a Book/Brain chart that describes the thinking Nora had done in *Loser* (also see Appendix 3).

I often create a Book/Brain chart first with the whole class during a read-aloud or shared reading, and then with individual students during conferences. That way, students are familiar with the format. But whether a Book/Brain chart has been created with a whole class, a small group, or an individual student, it's vital that it is made side by side with students, coconstructed from *their* reading experiences, not from ours. This is the difference between naming and explaining. I named something I noticed Nora did—her thinking—in one particular moment in a text and then framed it in a larger context of how texts work and how thinking works.

Instructing students by cocreating charts from their thinking is a form of what psychology researchers call attentional following. *Attentional following* is a term that emerged from research that compared infants whose mothers paid attention to what they paid attention to and infants whose mothers directed their attention away from something they were attending to. Those infants whose mothers practiced attentional following were found to have increased levels on a variety of learning measures. Those infants whose mothers practiced "attentional leading" showed lower levels of learning (Dunham, Dunham, and Curwin 1993). Gordon Wells's studies around the acquisition of language in young children reach similar conclusions. He found that parents who believed that "instruction and correction [were] necessary for language learning . . . fail[ed] to pick up and respond to cues from the child and, as a result, they actually ma[d]e it more difficult for the child to learn" (Wells 2009, 55). This is because those parents did not take into account that "children are active constructors of their own knowledge" (72) and that learning is the "collaborative construction of meaning" (113).

If, during my conference with Nora, I had focused on one of the many things she had *not* comprehended (the phrase *jungle cat grumble*, for example), my teaching would have been a form of "instruction and correction" or explaining rather than naming (for example, how authors sometimes use figurative language to get a mood across). Whatever I said by way of that explanation could have had any number of effects; for instance, it could have gone in one ear and out the other or it could have become a label Nora toted around, something she might have been able to identify but not necessarily something she had a deep understanding of or something that would help her develop a deep understanding of reading. If we want students to learn what we teach, which means internalizing it in ways they will be able to apply and transfer to other contexts, we need to start our teaching from the nexus of their thinking, paying attention to what they are paying attention to. Noticing and naming students' thinking, and charting it by way of a Book/Brain chart, is one way we can practice attentional following in our classrooms.

What About Students Who Aren't Doing Anything Well?

Much of the teaching I describe in the previous sections hinges on the teacher's recognizing and building off something a student is already doing well. I can hear your next question, though, because teachers ask it all the time: What about students who aren't doing anything well? What then? How do we access "and" and "because" messages for those students?

I have to say, Nora was one of those students. Her deficits—what she was *not* understanding—hit me in the face as I conferred with her. What helped me see what she was doing well was that I continually asked her how she knew what she knew and what textual clues she was using to give her information. If we can situate ourselves to focus not on what a student is getting or not getting and focus instead on what they are *doing*, we are often able to see that they are already problem solving in ways we would not have otherwise been able to notice. When we make the simple adjustment in our conferences to focus on how our students know what they know rather than on what they know, we are more likely to shine a light on the yearning that our students are doing rather than measuring how many inches their heels are off the floor.

But just to assure you that this is, indeed, possible, let's look at another conference using a simpler text.

Here's a second-grade student, Daniel, reading the pages of *Frog and Toad Are Friends* by Arnold Lobel (1970) that we looked at in Chapter 2.

DB: So, Daniel, what's going on here on this page?

Daniel: Frog is running up the path and knocks on the front door and a voice says, *"Blah."*

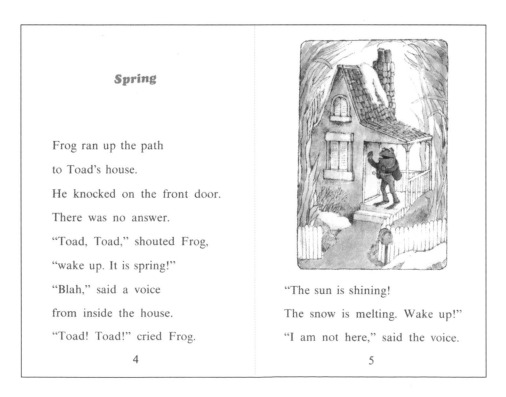

It seemed that Daniel was picking out a few sentences to hand me in answer to my question rather than rephrasing his comprehension. This happens a lot with struggling students: they reread rather than retell. I was concerned but thought I'd ask a few follow-up questions. I decided to repeat what Daniel said, not only to buy some time while I thought about my next steps, but also to demonstrate an active listening move, which is important for students.

DB: OK, so Frog is running up the path, knocks on the door, and a voice says, *"Blah."*

I thought to ask another question, then, that would help me see some of his comprehension better:

DB: Who do you think is saying, *"Blah"*?
Daniel: A ghost.

You could have knocked me over with a feather. How on earth did this child get this idea—and what was I going to do about it? Should I try to turn his attention to the textual clues that let *me* know this is Toad and not a ghost? Should I remind him to stay within "the four corners of the text," as David Coleman, one of the authors of the Common Core State Standards, has urged (2012, 4)? Should I recommend he move down a level? Or should I just say, "OK, let's see," and have him read on? I decided to rely on my standard question that attempts to get at how he got that thinking rather than what he was thinking:

DB: What made you think that, Daniel?
Daniel: [Points to the picture.] The house looks haunted.
DB: Ahh!

He was actually kind of right; perhaps he was using his background knowledge—possibly from movies—to bring meaning to this text. I wanted to see if that was the only clue he was using.

DB: Any other clues?
Daniel: Yes. Frog is crying. [Points to the phrase *Frog cried.*]

This was important information for me. I could see Daniel's thinking and perhaps teach from there. Again, I bought some time to collect my thoughts by repeating what he said.

DB: I see. So the house looks haunted and Frog is crying and that makes you think it's maybe a ghost saying, *"Blah."*

Daniel: [Nods and starts to turn the page.]

I felt I had a choice here: I could say something along the lines of "Let's see" and allow him to turn the page. But this would have been rather implicit, perhaps even vague, teaching around predicting and revising a prediction. It seemed that Daniel needed something more. He needed to stay more focused on the text and use more than one or two textual clues to help him comprehend. To do this, I could have him reread the page and reconsider each line. But that felt like I was pinning my teaching on his ability to suddenly see these words in a different light. If he didn't, then what was I going to do? I envisioned a trap in which I would find myself prompting him to comprehend what I was comprehending. This would be focusing my instruction on what he was getting or not getting rather than on what he was doing. So what was he doing, I wondered, and how could I build instruction from there? I jumped in to try to articulate what I had seen Daniel do:

DB: Before we read on, can I tell you what I noticed you did? This is a tricky part of this text. The author doesn't come right out and tell us who's saying, *"Blah"* here, right? It just says, *a voice.* It's like the author wants us to turn the page and find out whose voice it is—like a mystery. But still the author is planting clues that help you think about who *might* be saying, *"Blah."*

And you did exactly what the author wants you to do: You put clues together. You looked at the picture and you looked at these words, *Frog cried*, and put those clues together, like a puzzle.

That's exactly what a reader has to do when a writer doesn't come right out and tell us something—we have to put clues together. I can really see you did that here.

I diagrammed this on a piece of paper (Figure 3.3) to attempt to make it more visible to Daniel.

Figure 3.3
A diagram to help Daniel see how he put two clues together to make an inference

House looks haunted
+ cried Frog
————————————
= Ghost is saying 'blah!'

DB: I bet you can keep doing that, keep putting more clues together as you keep reading. So let's turn the page and see if we get more pieces we can fit together for our puzzle about who's saying, *"Blah."*

We turn the page.

Frog walked into the house.

It was dark.

All the shutters were closed.

"Toad, where are you?" called Frog.

"Go away," said the voice

from a corner of the room.

Toad was lying in bed.

6

He had pulled all the covers

over his head.

Frog pushed Toad out of bed.

He pushed him out of the house

and onto the front porch.

Toad blinked in the bright sun.

"Help!" said Toad.

"I cannot see anything."

7

Daniel: Oh. It's Toad!

DB: Wow! That's a change in your thinking! What made you think that?

Daniel: It shows him in bed.

DB: Great. You're using a clue in the picture just like you did before. Let's read the words and see if there are even more clues you can add to your thinking.

Daniel: [Reads.]

DB: Any more clues?

Daniel: It says, *Toad was lying in bed.*

DB: What does that tell you?

Daniel: That he doesn't feel like getting up.

DB: Wow! Do the words and pictures come right out and say that Toad doesn't feel like getting up?

Daniel: No.

DB: And do the words and pictures come right out and say that Toad is saying, "*Blah*"?

Daniel: No.

DB: But you knew, didn't you? You knew because you looked really closely at *some* of the clues on the first page. Then when you turned the page you got *more* clues from the pictures and then even more clues from the words. All those clues helped you realize you had to change your thinking. That's reading!

I returned to the diagram, showing Daniel how, when he put more clues together, he moved from "maybe" to "ah-ha" thinking (Figure 3.4).

I have now named for Daniel something about how texts work—that authors don't come right out and tell readers things but rather reveal them through the story. I have also illustrated two types of thinking readers do as a result: (1) add details together like clues in order to figure out what the author isn't saying directly; and (2) draft and revise the ideas, inferences, or hunches we develop from those clues. I did not make a Book/Brain chart with Daniel, since I had already diagrammed his thinking with him, but if I had, it could have looked something like the one in Figure 3.5.

I decided to do this teaching rather than, say, teaching him to infer about how characters are feeling, because this was where his attention was already focused. He was already using clues to figure out something the text doesn't state directly—thinking that, if extended, would help him be a more successful reader. In the words of my yoga teacher, he was yearning toward that thinking. My teaching move consisted only of highlighting his thinking and framing it around how texts work so that he could do that thinking with greater awareness and consistency.

Figure 3.4
Adding on to the diagram to help Daniel see how he revised his thinking by putting more clues together

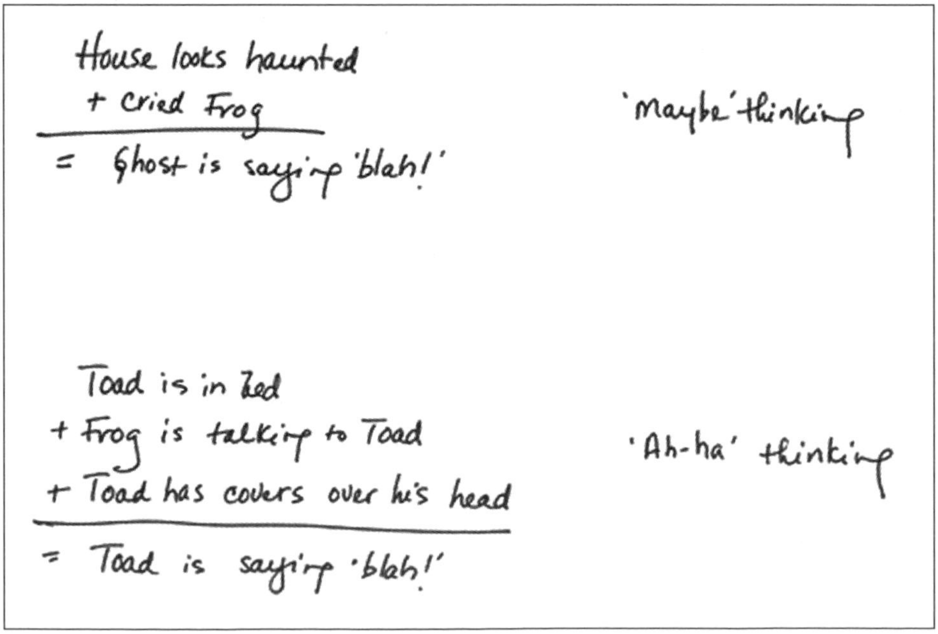

House looks haunted
+ Cried Frog
_____
= Ghost is saying 'blah!'

'maybe' thinking

Toad is in bed
+ Frog is talking to Toad
+ Toad has covers over his head
_____
= Toad is saying 'blah!'

'Ah-ha' thinking

Figure 3.5 Book/Brain chart filled in from conference with Daniel

How Texts Work (Book) ⟷	How Thinking Works (Brain)
Sometimes authors don't come right out and tell us information	We put clues together to think about "maybe" answers

We read on to put more clues together and turn our "maybe" thinking into "ah-ha" thinking |

I could have stopped the conference there, but I found myself itching to return to that first page with Daniel. Although he had read the words fluently, it seemed he had actually done very little thinking as he read. This was evident not just from his weak retelling but also from the fact that he used only two clues—the picture clue about the house and the phrase *Frog cried*—to make an inference about who was saying, *"Blah."* Even then it seemed he did so only because I had prompted him. I wasn't confident that he was doing much on his own beyond reading words. Knowing that this might be too much for one conference, I dove in nonetheless:

DB: So, Daniel, now that we're pretty sure this *voice* belongs to Toad, and now that we know readers figure out tricky texts by putting clues together, let's go back to the first page and see if we can see *other* clues the author might have slipped in that might hint that the voice could belong to Toad.

Daniel: [Reads the first page again.]

DB: Any clues you notice this time that might hint that this could be Toad's voice?

Daniel: Here. [Points to *"Toad, Toad," cried Frog.*]

Aware that this sentence contained the same phrase Daniel had isolated on his first read to mean that Frog was crying out of fear of a ghost, I wanted to make sure I was following him.

DB: Can you read it for me?

Daniel: *"Toad, Toad," cried Frog.*

DB: What does that show you?

Daniel: That Frog wants to play with Toad.

DB: Whoa, whoa, whoa. You're thinking so fast now, I can't keep up. How does that sentence tell you that Frog wants to play with Toad? The text doesn't say that, does it?

Daniel: No.

DB: So what makes you think that?

Daniel: Frog is running to Toad's house and he's saying *Toad! Toad!* because he's happy it's spring but Toad is still asleep.

I start making a new diagram as Daniel speaks (Figure 3.6):

DB: Daniel, look at the thinking you've done now! You're not just putting a few clues together to figure out who's saying, *"Blah"* but you put that part together with these other parts, which helped you think about how Frog is feeling and why. That's really tricky work! Does the author come right out and say, "Frog wants to play and he's happy that it's spring?"

Daniel: No.

DB: No! He's *showing* you through clues. And you paid attention to those clues, not just one or two, but *all* of them, and you added them together to help you do that important thinking work.

I left that conference grateful I had pushed on. Daniel surprised me no end with his capacity for inferring, causing me to think of the many times I have heard teachers bemoaning that their students can't infer. Perhaps it's

Figure 3.6
A diagram to help Daniel see how he put more clues together to make a revised inference

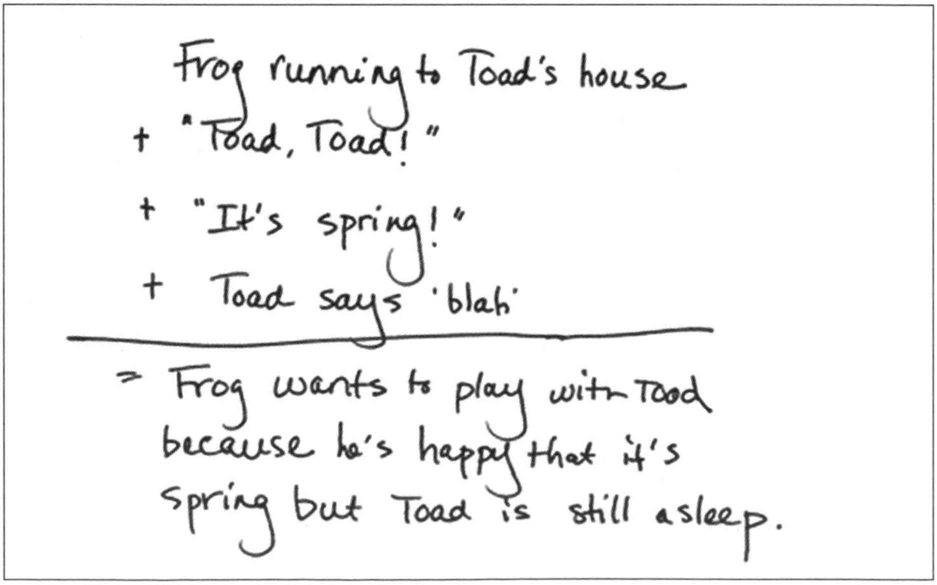

Frog running to Toad's house
+ "Toad, Toad!"
+ "It's spring!"
+ Toad says 'blah'
―――――――――――――――――
= Frog wants to play with Toad because he's happy that it's spring but Toad is still asleep.

not that they can't; perhaps they don't know how. Or, like the six-year-old soccer players who didn't realize what spreading out on the field would allow them to do, perhaps our students don't know why to infer and what the payoff can be.

Once again, if I was only looking at what Daniel was or wasn't getting, I would most likely have concluded that he wasn't inferring. But he was. He was doing what Marie Clay calls "partially correct" work (Clay 1991). Positioning myself to notice his approximations was what enabled me to teach him to see the payoff—which then enabled him to infer more accurately and consistently.

What It Means to Teach

You can see from my conferences with Daniel and Nora that my teaching is not about filling each student with information but about noticing and naming what they are already doing. This goes against many traditional notions we have about what it means to teach. The dictionary, for one, defines *teach* as "to explain" or "give information." And from my experience, when most nonteachers hear the word *teacher* they seem to think of someone at the front of a room talking at students. Most of us in the profession know that schools, classrooms, and teachers have progressed and moved away from these stereotypes. We know that classrooms aren't usually organized in rows and that very few teachers stand in front of a class talking at students. Yet when it comes to conferences, teachers still predominantly hunker down with a student, research a little to figure out what the student needs, and then proceed to explain or give information about what to do and how to do it. It's true that we're sitting beside students and having conversations about their independent reading books, but we might as well be standing in front of a classroom speaking to rows of silent students.

To rectify this, we need to expand our understanding of the term *teach* as part of a conference. We shouldn't only be thinking about *what* to teach; we also have to consider *how* to teach. As Jerome Bruner reminds us, "Pedagogy is never innocent. It is a medium that carries its own message" (1996, 63). If my job is to teach a student to recognize how she has been a problem solver in a text, I have to formulate my teaching to set the student up to be a problem solver. I can't be the problem solver for her. If I identify a problem the student is having in the text, hold out a solution, and show the student a strategy for working toward that solution, I will have done all the work in that conference.

We cannot do this *for* our students or *to* our students, but rather side by side, *with* them, engaged in a process of deep noticing in order to name. In my conference with Nora, I did not come armed with an agenda or a teaching point but, rather, discovered something about her as a reader by noticing what she was doing inside the pages of a text. With another reader doing something different inside those same pages, my conference would have been different—about word choice or imagery, for example ("Why do you think this author is using all these cat words to describe this car?"), or the character or point of view ("How do you think Donald feels about delivering mail with his father? Why? How do you know?"). Any of those conferences would have led me to name a different aspect of how texts work—how imagery can advance an idea or convey a tone, for example, or how characters are developed over time, or how point of view impacts a reader—and to name a different way that readers think in texts.

A conference is not a delivery system for a teaching point; it is a teachable moment in and of itself. Here, while a student is reading, is our opportunity to notice how she is constructing meaning. Here is our opportunity to show her how to turn that meaning into knowledge, knowledge about the process of reading and knowledge about how texts work.

TOOLBOX ➤ HOW TO TEACH BY NOTICING AND NAMING

- Notice the thinking you see the student doing and the behaviors you see the student using as she reads.
  - Ask the student "how-do-you-know" questions to help you "see" her thinking.
- Name back to the student what you notice by describing what you saw him do—his thinking.
- Name what you think that means he knows about how texts work.
  - Try to generalize what you notice so it is applicable to all (or most) texts.
- Think about how you can build upon what the student is already doing or approximating.

In Nora's conference:

I named:
- The knowledge about texts she was using ("So you know that the names of places are often capitalized.")

- The behaviors she exhibited ("I love the way you're rereading to try to figure that out.")
- The thinking I saw her doing ("You're carrying information from the previous page.")

  I built on:

- Her knowledge about how texts work ("Authors don't just throw random things into the middle of a story.")
- What she was already doing ("You did this there, now do it here.")

In Daniel's conference:

  I named:

- The knowledge about texts he was using ("The author doesn't come right out and tell us"; "the author wants us to turn the page"; "the author is planting clues.")
- The thinking I saw him doing ("You put clues together"; "you looked really closely.")

  I built on:

- His knowledge about how texts work ("Authors don't come right out and say how [characters] feel and why.")
- What he was already doing ("You got more clues and realized you had to change your thinking"; "you paid attention to . . . all [the clues] and added them together.")

Book/Brain Charts

- Create Book/Brain charts from what you notice and name if you think they will help your students keep track of their thinking and apply it to other books.
- The Book/Brain chart is a tool, not a product. It is meant to concretize the notice-and-name work you've done with a student.
- The Book/Brain chart is based on something you notice and name with the student *as* she reads. By definition, noticing and naming is teaching done side-by-side with students.
    - I do not carry prepared charts with me as I approach students, nor do I use the same charts from class to class or school to school.
    - For the purpose of time, I sometimes make a chart *after* I confer with a student, but it is based on specific work I've noticed that student doing and serves as a kind of summary of the conference.
- I use Book/Brain charts in a combination of individual, small-group, and whole-class scenarios—whenever I am noticing and naming.

    ○ Some teachers like to create a Book/Brain chart for every student. They create these charts after a research conference and then add to them as they do follow-up conferences (see Chapter 4). Students keep these charts in their reading folders.

    ○ Other teachers find it onerous to create a chart for every student. They prefer to use a written chart only for whole-class work in the read-aloud or shared reading. During conferences, they might frame the work they see individual students doing during their conferences around the whole-class Book/Brain chart, but they don't actually write out a chart for each student.

    ○ I suggest a middle path. Some students greatly benefit from having a visual reminder about a reading conference, especially because reading work is highly abstract. Others may not refer to it at all, and it will become just another piece of paper cluttering their already disorganized folders and desks.

- Above all, the Book/Brain chart needs to remain a tool that helps you and your students be more aware of some of the invisible work of reading. Feel free to tweak the format of the chart and the frequency of use.

    ○ A K–1 teacher, for example, thought the two-column format would be too text heavy for her students and so preferred to use a web format. After reading aloud and discussing a picture book with her whole class, we summarized the "Book" part of their understanding into the middle bubble and placed all the "Brain" work we noticed the students did around it (Figure 3.7).

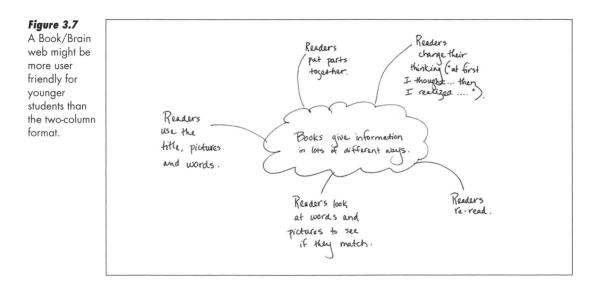

Figure 3.7
A Book/Brain web might be more user friendly for younger students than the two-column format.

TEACHING SMARTER

*Stepping Students
Up to Do More
Complex Thinking in
Independent Reading*

*You'll be sort of surprised what there is to be found once you go beyond
Z and start poking around!*

—Dr. Seuss

While high expectations have always been an essential part of learning, expectations under the Common Core State Standards have taken on a whole new tenor. Teachers are under increased pressure to push students—and push them hard. In 2005, for example, students were expected to read books on a C level by the end of kindergarten. That level has now gone up to D. Similarly, for first grade it was I and now it's J (Fountas and Pinnell 2012). In the Common Core materials, exemplar texts have been chosen to illustrate the new expectations. *Sarah, Plain and Tall* by Patricia MacLachlan is one such text for grades two and three. Here is its opening page:

> *"Did Mama sing every day?" asked Caleb. "Every-single-day?" He sat close to the fire, his chin in his hand. It was dusk, and the dogs lay beside him on the warm hearthstones.*
>
> *"Every-single-day," I told him for the second time this week. For the twentieth time this month. The hundredth time this year? And the past few years?*
>
> *"And did Papa sing, too?"*
>
> *"Yes. Papa sang, too. Don't get so close, Caleb. You'll heat up."*
>
> *He pushed his chair back. It made a hollow scraping sound on the hearthstones, and the dogs stirred. Lottie, small and black, wagged her tail and lifted her head. Nick slept on.* (1985, 3)

No doubt there are some second and third graders who can read this passage, meaning they can decode most of the words in order to understand the information it's conveying—basically who is in the scene and what is going on (though when I have read this scene with adults in workshops, there have been some interesting disagreements about whether the *Nick* in the last sentence is a dog or a baby). But there is more to reading than simply figuring out the who and the what. To truly understand a text, as Vicki Vinton and I explored in *What Readers Really Do*, a reader needs to be considering from the get-go what the details signify and how they are adding up (Barnhouse and Vinton 2012).

This early in the text, of course, we have no clue about how anything might be adding up, so we ask a lot of questions: we may wonder, for example, why this character Caleb is so interested in whether his mother and father sang every day, or what the relationship is between Caleb and the unnamed narrator. We may wonder where the mother and father are and why the narrator says, *For the twentieth time this month. The hundredth time this year? And the past few years?* We may have already developed a few ideas or drawn conclusions from the details but from our past experience with texts, we know we are likely to get more information as we keep reading and will therefore be able to confirm or have to revise our thinking accordingly.

Clearly, a fluent, experienced reader does this work instantaneously, maybe even unconsciously. Just as clearly, many second graders are not yet ready to do this much work on one page. Granted the CCSS assure teachers that the levels published are goals to be attained "by the end of the year," and that some students may need "scaffolding . . . at the high end of the range" (Common Core State Standards 2012a). But the classrooms I work in, and probably yours as well, are populated with students like Daniel, the second grader from the last chapter who read *Frog and Toad*. How much scaffolding will the Daniels and Noras in our classrooms need to meet these expectations?

Rethinking the Staircase of Text Complexity

The grade-level expectations written into the Common Core State Standards were written in response to what was viewed as a "gap" between the rising complexity of "reading demands for college, career, and citizenship" and the decreasing complexity of texts that students were "exposed to" in school (Common Core State Standards 2012a). The formula describing and measuring text complexity that I talked about in the introduction (see page 6) was created in response to this perceived gap and teachers are being urged to make sure their students are "exposed" to texts that match this "complexity staircase" so they can reach "college and career readiness levels" (Common Core State Standards 2012a).

While the information provided in Appendix A about text complexity is not *un*helpful for teachers, it's also not exactly helpful. Its emphasis, unfortunately, is solely on the texts. It is the texts that make up the staircase; it's the text that needs to be taught. This emphasis on texts encourages—some might even say requires—teachers to take their eyes off their students. But as any amateur Ping-Pong player knows, taking your eye off the ball is a surefire way to miss a shot entirely. So, too, with teaching. If we focus on where students need to be without paying attention to where they are, we will surely fail.

Irene Fountas and Gay Su Pinnel remind us that "The construction of systems 'in the head' is unique for each student." Therefore, teachers should "notice each student's precise literacy behaviors and provide appropriate teaching that supports students in developing their systems of strategic actions" (Fountas and Pinnell 2012, 5). The noticing-and-naming work described in previous chapters allows us to see those systems—a student's thinking on the page—as well as the relative complexity of the text that the student is reading. If we don't keep our eyes on our students, we won't be able to determine how best to support and extend their learning. Instead of teaching our students, we will be pushing, pulling, and dragging them up the text-complexity staircase.

Keeping our eyes on our students doesn't mean keeping our students where they are. They do need to become better readers, thinkers, and learners.

So how can we both notice and name what students are doing *and* extend their learning to approach increasingly high expectations?

Let's answer that question by rethinking the staircase metaphor that the Standards emphasize. Rather than looking at complexity only through the lens of a text, let's look at complexity as an intersection between the text and the reader. At the bottom of the staircase is a reader doing simple thinking in a simple text. At the top of the staircase is a reader doing complex thinking in a complex text (Figure 4.1). In between are readers doing simple thinking in complex texts and complex thinking in simple texts. My goal as a teacher is to help each student expand from where they are so they can do complex thinking in texts that are complex for them.

It's important to note that this staircase of text-and-reader complexity is not linear. This is because complexity is a relative term—what's complex for one reader might be simple for another—and also because reading is such a complex process. One text might have simple and complex parts, or a reader might be doing simple thinking sometimes and complex thinking at other times. Nonetheless, a spectrum can help us design instruction that meets high expectations but also keeps our students at the center of our classroom practice.

Using this spectrum, I would place Nora somewhere in the Simple Reading/Complex Texts range. She was clearly reading simply: she was decoding words and following some of the basic action in the scene she was reading from *Loser*, but she was not following all the action, nor did she seem to be building meaning from any of the details she noticed or connecting them to any of the previous pages she had read. Even though *Loser* would probably not be considered a complex text for fifth grade by the standards of the Common Core, I would label the text complex for Nora because the page she was reading did not explicitly state what meaning the details carried or what that part had to do with the rest of the book. To fully understand this scene, therefore, a reader had to infer by carrying and connecting information across many pages and chapters.

Figure 4.1
Staircase of text-and-reader complexity

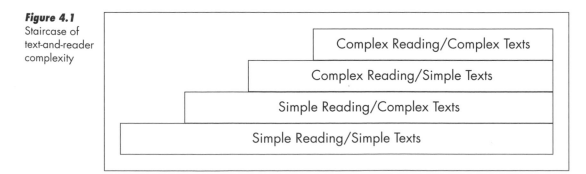

| Complex Reading/Complex Texts |
| Complex Reading/Simple Texts |
| Simple Reading/Complex Texts |
| Simple Reading/Simple Texts |

Let's step inside some classrooms to meet a few other students, examine where they may be on this spectrum, and think about instructional next steps that can help extend their learning.

Up the Staircase: From Simple Work in Simple Texts to Complex Work in Simple Texts

Jared was a fourth grader with special needs in a Collaborative Team Teaching (CTT) class at a school in Queens. The school used a highly structured basal-type curriculum in reading, with a skill of the week, ability-based guided reading groups, and largely scripted materials. Before I conferred with Jared, I met with his teacher, who told me they had been working on inferring as the skill of the week using a formula provided in the textbook:

What the text says + Prior knowledge + Consider what makes sense = Inference

If you have read *What Readers Really Do*, you know that Vicki Vinton and I have taken issue with this method of teaching inferring (Barnhouse and Vinton 2012). It seems vague at best (what does "what makes sense" mean to a child, and what "prior knowledge" should a student use, exactly, and when?). Additionally, it seems inaccurate. After years of research conferences in which I have tried to listen to how students know what they know in texts, I've concluded that readers who infer are actually doing so by making what Vicki and I call "within-text connections." Connecting or adding details together helps readers infer information that is not stated directly but rather revealed indirectly through action, dialogue, and description, and also helps readers consider why characters might be doing or saying something. We saw Daniel, in Chapter 3, doing this exact thinking as he read *Frog and Toad*. If I want to teach students to infer, therefore, I usually teach them to ask why questions and to draft answers to those questions by connecting details.

When I sat down with Jared, he bragged to me about how much he loved to read. "Great," I replied. "What are you reading today?" He held out one of the books in The Littles series. "I've read them all!" he said proudly. When I asked him to turn to the part he was reading today, he opened to page 7.

"Granny's sad about something—that's what I think," Lucy said. She sat beside Tom on the mattress.

"I wonder what," Tom said.

"Maybe we can make her happy again if we try," said Lucy.

"Hey!" Tom hopped to his feet on the spongy mattress. "It's almost dinnertime. Let's see what the Biggs are eating." The tiny boy somersaulted twelve times to the end of the mattress. He jumped to the floor of the attic.

"That's not fair—somersaulting makes me dizzy!" said Lucy. "You know that. I can't do it. I give up!" She climbed down from the mattress and ran to catch up with Tom. (Peterson 1972)

He read with perfect fluency and expression, particularly emphasizing bits of dialogue (*"Hey!" "That's not fair!"* and *"I give up!"*).

DB: I can tell that you love to read, Jared. You read with such expression.

Jared: Thanks.

DB: So tell me, when you read these lines [*"Hey!"* and *"That's not fair!"*], how did you know to make your voice sound that way?

Jared looked at me without comprehending so I rephrased.

DB: You said those words like this. [Echoes how he read them, with great enthusiasm and excitement.] How did you know to do that instead of saying them in just a normal voice?

Jared: Oh. The exclamation point. It helped me.

DB: How did the exclamation point help you?

Jared: It means they're excited.

DB: Oh, so the exclamation point is telling you that the characters are excited here?

Jared: Yeah.

I was thinking here that Jared was inferring but was using only the most basic clues to help him do so. I decided to push him a little.

DB: Are there any other clues that help you know how the characters might be feeling?

Jared: Yes, the words helped me.

DB: Which words helped you?

Jared: *"That's not fair!"* Those words. When someone says that it's like, "That's not fair!" [Voices the words with expression again.]

Here I could see that Jared was probably using some of his life experience, or "prior knowledge" as the textbook called it, to help him infer. It was a start, and I decided to notice and name the work he was doing before I attempted to extend his understanding of how to do this more complexly.

DB: That's great inferring, Jared. I know you've been working on that in class and I see you're really doing that here. The text doesn't come right out and tell you how the characters are feeling. It doesn't say, "Lucy was excited." But you know they're excited because of *what* they're saying and also *how* they're saying it, which the author tells you through the exclamation points.

Jared: Yeah.

DB: Let's look at another sentence. Here. *"Granny's sad about something— that's what I think."* This is a little trickier, because it doesn't have any exclamation points. What do you think Lucy might be feeling when she says that?

Jared: She's feeling that her Granny is sad.

DB: How do you know that?

Jared: The words say it.

DB: I see. Yes. The words do say it.

At this point I felt myself in a little bit of a bind. Lucy *is* saying that her Granny is sad but that seems to be the simplest reading of that sentence. What Lucy herself is feeling is not stated. However, since Jared seemed to be a very literal thinker, I didn't quite know how to tease out this subtlety so I thought I'd come at my point through exploring why questions.

DB: Do you have any idea why Lucy said that, why she thinks her Granny is sad?

Jared: [Quiet.]

I was unsure if Jared wasn't responding because he didn't know the answer to my question or because he didn't understand my question. I tried again.

DB: Is this the first time Granny is mentioned in the book?

Jared: No. Here.

Jared turned back to pages 4 and 5 and read a passage that describes Tom, Lucy, Uncle Pete, and Granny Little in a room together having a conversation.

Granny Little is described as *rocking slowly back and forth* in a chair. Tom, Lucy, and Uncle Pete notice that she doesn't respond to what they are talking about. While Uncle Pete dismisses her as being hard of hearing, Tom is more worried: *"Granny's not even* trying *to listen. That's the trouble!"* (Peterson 1972, 5).

DB: Oh. I like how you remembered that Granny was in this scene, Jared. That means you're really holding onto the story. So from reading this page, do you get any idea about why Lucy said what she did on page 7, about why she thinks her Granny is sad?
Jared: No.

I recognized here that I was prompting Jared pretty heavily. The telltale sign was that I was itching for a specific answer from him; I wanted him to say that Lucy thought Granny was sad on page 7 because of how she was behaving on page 4. I could have continued this conference in such a manner, perhaps even pointing to one of the lines on page 4 that I recognized as meaningful and asking Jared how he thought Granny was feeling here. I could even have resorted to the textbook's approach to inferring, which would have involved asking him how he might feel if his grandmother were sad.

But I needed to teach Jared, not the text, and was worried that further prompting would merely teach the text. What Jared needed to learn to do was to think more complexly. He needed to learn that readers don't just make line-by-line inferences but do so across pages, often by connecting line-by-line inferences and by considering why questions. This seemed like big work and not something I was prepared to give a little mini-lecture on right then and there. I therefore decided to hold off on the teaching portion of this conference and plan more carefully how best to help Jared do this work. I also imagined that there were a few other students in Jared's class who could use a similar lesson, and tucked the idea of a small group into the back of my thinking.

In the meantime, though, I wanted to lay the foundation for the work to come. If I could help Jared see the thinking he was already doing and what that thinking allowed him to know and do in this text, he would be on solid ground to think more complexly. I decided to use the noticing-and-naming techniques discussed in Chapter 3 to help me do this. First, I named something he knew about how texts work and then I named something I saw him do as a problem solver.

DB: I see from your reading today, Jared, that you know a lot about books. You know that authors don't always come right out and tell readers everything, particularly how characters are feeling. You know they use clues, like the exclamation marks you noticed. That helped you understand the characters more deeply here.

We'll continue working on this together, looking at clues authors use that help a reader understand characters more deeply—how they're feeling and also maybe why they're doing what they're doing and saying what they're saying.

I decided to hold off on noticing and naming the other thinking I saw Jared do; namely, carry information about the grandmother from page 4 to page 7. I didn't want to overwhelm him but will certainly come back to this point at another time.

Next Steps: Infer How Characters Are Feeling by Using More Implicit Signals

During a planning period I had with Jared's teacher after this conference, we talked about possible next instructional steps. Since I believe that any journey up the staircase of text complexity needs to start with what a student is already doing well, we tried to articulate what we saw Jared doing well and composed a Book/Brain chart (see Chapter 3) about his thinking (Figure 4.2). I find Book/Brain charts to be helpful tools in embarking on the process of moving students up to do more complex work since they make visible for students the thinking they are already doing.

Figure 4.2 Chart of the thinking Jared was doing in *The Littles Give a Party*

How Texts Work (Book)	**How Thinking Works (Brain)**
Sometimes authors don't come right out and tell us how characters are feeling	We think about how characters might be feeling by putting clues together: • what they say • punctuation
Characters are sometimes introduced early in the book and don't come back until later pages	We hold on to what we've already read

Because I was not going to return to this classroom for several weeks, the teacher planned to do a quick check-in conference with Jared during the next day's independent reading period. During that check-in she handed him the Book/Brain chart we had created, stating that this was the thinking we had seen him do in the previous day's conference. On a subsequent day when she had a few more minutes with him, she planned to ask some follow-up questions about the pages he had since read: Had he come across any other places where the author didn't come right out and tell the reader how a character was feeling? How had he figured out what they might be feeling? Jared continued to use some of the same strategies he had when I conferred with him, namely what characters say and the punctuation the author uses, and the teacher affirmed this work.

The teacher also began to shift the emphasis of her whole-class teaching during read-aloud and shared reading. She was no longer teaching inferring as an isolated skill but something the students did continually as they read, connecting details within a text and asking and answering why questions about what the characters were doing, saying, and thinking (Barnhouse and Vinton 2012). During this work, she kept a close eye on Jared. She then had an additional follow-up conference with him during which she recognized that he had made an inference based on what a character was doing and how others were treating him. She added those strategies (in boldface type) to his Book/Brain chart (Figure 4.3).

Figure 4.3 Adding to Jared's Book/Brain chart from the thinking he did in follow-up conferences

How Texts Work (Book) ⟷	How Thinking Works (Brain)
Sometimes authors don't come right out and tell us how characters are feeling	We think about how characters might be feeling by putting clues together: • what they say • punctuation • **what they do** • **how others treat them**
Characters are sometimes introduced early in the book and don't come back until later pages	We hold on to what we've already read

Next Steps: Infer How Characters Are Feeling by Connecting Details Across Pages

Despite the good work that Jared was doing and the plan his teacher and I had put into place, he still had a long way to go. For one, he wasn't reading on grade level (*The Littles Give a Party* is an M text, according to Fountas and Pinnell (2012) and fourth graders should be between Q and S). But even in texts that Jared read and reread, such as *The Littles Give a Party*, he needed to do more complex thinking. Line-by-line inferring is important and Jared could certainly get better at that, but ultimately he needed to learn to think across pages and internalize *why* questions as he read.

By the time I returned to his class, Jared had started another book, *Marvin Redpost: Kidnapped at Birth?* by Louis Sachar. Before I had him read, I rifled through his reading folder and found the Book/Brain chart the teacher had given him some weeks back. It was not clear how he had used it on his own, but I brought it out as a visual reminder of the earlier work he had done. I then had him start reading from the page he was on, which was about halfway through the book:

> "Well, I suppose anything is possible," said Mrs. North.
> "I watched the news last night," said Stuart. "The King of Shampoo was on. They gave a number to call. I wrote it down."
> "Well there you go," said Mrs. North. "All you have to do is call that number."
> But at that moment, Marvin was feeling strangely sad.
> He was thinking about what Casey Happleton said. The real Marvin Redpost was dead. (Sachar 1992, 27–28)

As I went through my usual conference moves (see Chapter 1), asking Jared to explain what was going on and how he knew, he gave me a general retelling of the plot: Marvin thought he was kidnapped at birth and was really a prince.

DB: I see that you're holding on to the story, Jared. That's important work. Did you find yourself doing any of this inferring work as you read? [Gestures to the chart.]

Jared: Yeah. Here. [Points to the last line: *He was thinking about what Casey Happleton said. The real Marvin Redpost was dead.*]

DB: Tell me about that.

Jared: Marvin is thinking here. And he's feeling sad.

DB: OK. Can you show me where you got the idea that he was sad?

Jared: [Points to the words *thinking* and *feeling strangely sad.*]

This seemed like one of those instances where the textual clues were more explicit than not. I was not convinced that Jared would be ready for inferring from less explicit textual clues, let alone connecting clues across pages, but I jumped in nonetheless.

DB: Yes, I see. So you're inferring in order to pay attention to what the character is feeling. That's so important in a story.

Another reason that readers infer is that authors also don't always come out and tell us *why* characters are doing or saying things. Readers kind of have to figure that out by inferring. So can you think here about why Marvin might be feeling *strangely sad*? And why *strangely* sad? Why not just *sad*? What's strange about it?

Jared: I don't think Marvin wants to be prince.

This was an interesting statement. First of all, Jared used the word *think* and he was slightly tentative about it. This was very different from his previous talk about *The Littles Give a Party*, which had been very cut-and-dried. This indicated to me that he was actually puzzling something out, a way of thinking I credited to the shift in the read-aloud work the teacher had been doing. Additionally, I didn't see anything on the page that hinted that Marvin didn't want to be prince. This clued me in that Jared was indeed doing more complex thinking across pages.

DB: Oh? What makes you think that?

Jared: I don't think he's going to make the phone call.

DB: What phone call is that?

Jared: [Points to the line spoken by Mrs. North: *"All you have to do is call that number."*]

DB: So how does that help you think about why he's feeling *strangely sad*?

Jared: He wanted to be prince but now he doesn't.

DB: Really? Can you show me where he wanted to be prince?

Jared: [Starts to flip back pages but can't find what he's looking for.]

DB: Can you tell me what you're looking for?

Jared: He said he felt like Prince Robert and didn't like being called Marvin anymore.

DB: But now he doesn't want to be prince?

Jared: I don't think so.

Wow! Jared was doing a lot of thinking here: he was inferring around a character's feelings; he was noticing a change in a character; *and* he was making a prediction. Each of these actually involves inferring. He inferred about why Marvin was feeling *strangely sad* and then used that information to think ahead, not just about what might happen next but about what the character might do or not do based on his feelings. This is a more complex level of understanding than simply thinking about what will happen next. And it is so much more complex than the line-by-line inferring he had been doing in *The Littles Give a Party*. He had answered or was beginning to consider several why questions—why Marvin was *strangely sad* and why Marvin was changing his mind about wanting to be a prince—and he had done so by connecting information across pages.

The thinking I saw Jared doing in this conference involves aspects of a text that are often unstated—namely, character motivation and how characters change over time. To do this thinking, a reader needs to actively connect what is happening on one page to what has come before and what will most likely come later. The challenge I faced with Jared was explaining his amazing thinking to him in terms he could understand and apply to other texts.

I started by congratulating him and then attempted to help him visualize his thinking by sketching it. Figure 4.4 is a rendering of my attempt that I explained as I drew.

Figure 4.4 A diagram of the thinking that Jared was doing. The dot represents the words Jared was reading on page 28. The backward arrows indicate the information he's already read that he's using to answer his why question. The forward arrow represents how he thinks that information will impact the character's actions to come.

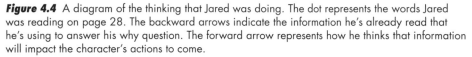

DB: Jared, the thinking you're doing is the thinking of a reader. You are reading a passage here, on page 28, and asking a why question: Why is Marvin feeling *strangely sad*?

In order to answer that question, you're using information you're getting from previous pages. You're also using that information to think ahead, to what the character might do in the future. That's reading— connecting details together to think deeply about why characters are doing what they're doing.

Later, during the planning period I had with the teacher, we added to Jared's Book/Brain chart, which the teacher returned to him the following day (Figure 4.5).

I asked Jared's teacher to keep a close eye on him through check-in conferences and during the whole-class reading. I particularly wanted to be sure that he was asking and trying to answer why questions as he read since he had done this work only when prompted by me. But since Jared had been made aware of the importance of why questions and since he saw the powerful thinking he had done when answering the why question I asked, I was

Figure 4.5 Jared's Book/Brain chart with his new thinking added in boldface type

How Texts Work (Book) ⟷	How Thinking Works (Brain)
Sometimes authors don't come right out and tell us how characters are feeling	We put clues together: • what they say • punctuation • what they do • how others treat them
Characters are sometimes introduced early in the book and don't come back until later pages	We hold on to what we've already read
Sometimes authors don't come right out and tell us why characters are doing or saying or thinking things	**We ask why questions and try to answer them by:** • **putting clues together from one page to another** • **paying attention to how characters change** • **thinking backward and forward as we read**

confident that with continued practice in independent reading and support during shared reading, he would indeed do this more complex thinking more independently.

When we want students to do more complex thinking in just-right texts, it's important that we help them see:

- the thinking they are already doing in texts they don't struggle with and are engaged in;
- how to do thinking that connects across pages, not just line by line;
- the importance of asking and answering *why* questions;
- the meaning that complex thinking allows the reader to make. It is not isolated work in skill books or computer programs but deep work across pages in books we are engaged in.

Up the Staircase: From Complex Work in Simple Texts to Complex Work in Complex Texts

Carlos, a fifth-grade student, was reading *Diary of a Wimpy Kid: The Ugly Truth* the day I did a research conference with him. He was on page 172:

> *I will say the whole episode has got me thinking. I've been waiting to hit my growth spurt or at least start growing some facial hair, but things have been kind of slow going.*
>
> *And now that Rowley's got a pimple, I'm kind of anxious to get things moving along.*
>
> *When I got home from school today, I checked myself in the mirror to see if anything seemed different. But everything looked exactly the same as it always does.* (Kinney 2010)

DB: So, Carlos, what does this first line mean? What is the *episode* the narrator is referring to?

Carlos: They watched a video about puberty.

DB: Where does it say that? How do you know?

Carlos: Back here. [Flips back to page 18 where there's a reference to the video they watched in class.]

DB: Oh. So the *episode* is the video they watched?

Carlos: Yeah.

DB: And this part about *anxious to get things moving along*, what do you think that means?

Carlos: Well, I'm not sure what *anxious* means but he wants to grow. He's getting impatient.

DB: That *is* what anxious means in this context: impatient. So why do you think he's feeling anxious or impatient?

Carlos: Because Rowley has a pimple and Gregg doesn't.

DB: [Laughs.] Last time I checked no one wanted a pimple. Why does Gregg want one?

Carlos: Because he wants to show it off to all the older kids.

DB: I notice that the text doesn't come right out and say that he wants to show it off. So how do you know that's what he's feeling here?

Carlos: Well, Rowley was showing off here [Flips to earlier pages.] and he wants to be friends with Rowley again so . . . .[Shrugs.]

DB: Carlos, do you know what you just did as a reader? You put all these details together—the detail about Rowley showing off plus the detail about Gregg wanting to be friends with Rowley—and that helped you know why, on this page, Gregg wanted a pimple and why's he's feeling impatient about it.

You're thinking about why characters are doing what they're doing and answering those why questions by putting all the details of the story together. I can almost see your brain doing that when you're flipping through the pages.

That's what inferring is: putting details together in order to help you think about why characters might be doing, saying, or thinking what they are.

This conference was a typical notice-and-name conference: I noticed thinking I saw Carlos doing and tried to name how he did that thinking and what that thinking allowed him to understand in his book. I used the academic term *inferring* since that was being taught explicitly in his class and he was aware of the word, but rather than just labeling his thinking I tried to specify *how* we was inferring as well as *why* he was inferring—something I will try to build on as he enters into more complex texts.

Next Steps: Connect Details Across Pages in a More Complex Text

In order to extend Carlos's learning, I felt I had a few options and wanted to talk with his teacher before settling on one. We huddled in a corner of the classroom while the students read independently and agreed that Carlos was doing complex work but thought perhaps he was doing so in a relatively simple text—at least simple for Carlos. The trick was to support him to do the same work—infer across pages by connecting details—in a more complex text. We thought a book with a few more characters as well as characters who faced multiple problems, not just one, might be an appropriate challenge for Carlos. At the same time we wanted to be sure that we didn't overwhelm him with the work of reading: the decoding and vocabulary couldn't be too onerous, the print not too small, the book not too long. And we wanted to be sure to keep him engaged in a character with whom he could identify. In other words, it had to be another boy story.

We took a quick look through the classroom library and thought that perhaps *There's a Boy in the Girls' Bathroom* by Louis Sachar might do the trick. The teacher knew another student, one of Carlos's friends, who might be able to partner up with Carlos as a kind of reading buddy. If they read the book at the same time, she thought, perhaps checking in with each other at intervals as they were reading, Carlos might be able to get through some of the vocabulary, check his comprehension, and keep his motivation high.

We drafted a quick Book/Brain chart (Figure 4.6) that would allow Carlos to hold on to the thinking we saw him do in the conference and help steer some of the work we hoped to see him do in a new book. In addition to the why thinking I saw Carlos do, I decided to add something to his chart

Figure 4.6 The beginnings of a Book/Brain chart describing Carlos's thinking

How Texts Work **(Book)** ⟷	**How Thinking Works** **(Brain)**
Authors don't come right out and tell us why characters are doing or saying or thinking things	We ask why questions as we read Sometimes we don't get answers to our why questions until we keep reading We put clues together to help us answer our why questions, thinking back to what we've already read
Sometimes there are words we don't know in books	We put clues together from the story to help us think about what the word could mean We substitute a word we think it means and see if that makes sense

about the work he had done around the word *anxious*. I knew a more complex text was likely to have more complex words and wanted Carlos to feel supported as he navigated these words. As I thought about how to describe this thinking to him, I realized that the way he had understood the word *anxious* was the exact same way he had understood the scene he had been reading: by putting clues together across pages. Often when we teach context clues to students around unknown words, we teach a very small context ("the words around the word"). But Carlos had used a much larger context—the same span of pages, in fact (from page 172 back to page 18) that had helped him do much of the why thinking that was essential to his comprehension around the characters.

The teacher and I approached Carlos again and showed him the chart of his thinking. We then asked him to be sure to check in with his teacher when he finished *Diary of a Wimpy Kid* so she could get him started on the Louis Sachar book. We planned to have frequent check-in conferences with Carlos to make sure his page-to-page reading didn't get too tiresome for him, and additionally planned to check in during some of the talk time he would have with his reading buddy, at the end of independent reading every day. We were confident, however, that asking, holding on to, and answering why questions was going to be productive work for him.

When we want students to do more complex thinking in more complex texts, it's important that we help them see:

- the thinking they have done in simpler texts;
- what that thinking has yielded—meaning, engagement, involvement with the characters—and therefore what to expect from another reading experience;
- that they can think across pages, not just sentences and paragraphs, to consider the meaning of unknown words;
- that they can get support through working with a partner or book buddy.

Up the Staircase: Sustaining Complex Thinking in Complex Texts

Alex was a third grader at a school in Brooklyn. His teacher was concerned that he was reading below the level of his peers. Additionally, she said he often had difficulty focusing during independent reading. The day I worked in his class, he was reading *Marvin Redpost: A Magic Crystal?* by Louis Sachar. The section he read from during our conference was on page 74:

> *Everybody cheered—except Casey, who couldn't, and Marvin, who didn't feel very cheerful.*
>
> *Lake Park was three blocks from Marvin's school. Everyone had to walk with a buddy. Marvin's buddy was Stuart. Nick and Warren walked right behind them.*
>
> *"Look, there's Casey," Marvin said. "Watch. I bet you she'll talk."*
> *Casey was buddies with Judy.*
> *"I don't care," said Stuart.*
> *"I don't care either," said Marvin.*
>
> *Mrs. North started out in front, but she dropped back until she was walking next to Judy and Casey.*
>
> *"Darn!" said Marvin. "Now she won't say anything with Mrs. North right there."*
> *"I don't care," said Stuart.*
> *"Me neither," said Marvin.* (Sachar 2000)

Alex's fluency was not perfect. He tripped over his words, self-corrected many times, substituted several words and skipped over others. For example, he read *Everyone walked with a buddy* instead of *Everyone had to walk with a buddy* and *Mrs. North stayed in front* instead of *Mrs. North started out in front*. He also pronounced *Casey* as if it were spelled *Cassey* and *Stuart* as if it was spelled *Start*. But keeping in mind that correcting is not teaching, I dove into my research.

DB: So tell me, Alex, why couldn't Casey cheer?
Alex: Casey couldn't cheer because of the magic crystal. But I think she was happy.

I could have asked two questions here: one about the magic crystal and one about the character being happy. I was afraid that if I asked about the magic crystal I might get a long plot retelling, the kind that doesn't necessarily help with insight into a student's thinking, so I chose to question Alex about the character being happy.

DB: What makes you think she's happy?
Alex: Everyone is happy.
DB: Why are they happy?
Alex: The teacher's giving them a treat. [Flips to the previous page and shows me where it says that the teacher is rewarding them for *working so nice and quietly.*]

DB: So why isn't Marvin feeling cheerful?

Alex: Because he just had a fight with Casey. He thinks Casey *can* talk and that she's just pretending.

DB: So how does that fight fit with this part when he says he doesn't care?

Alex: Oh, he *does* care. He just has to agree with his best friend.

DB: That's so interesting, Alex. Because the author doesn't come right out and say that. So how do you know that he really *does* care here?

Alex: Well, he keeps saying, *"I don't care"* [Flips to some earlier pages to show me.] but he only says it *after* Stuart says it. And also he keeps saying, *"I bet she'll talk."* I think he feels bad for what he did.

I thought about what I had seen Alex do. Like Carlos reading *Diary of a Wimpy Kid*, Alex was carrying the story with him, which helped him do all the inference work required on this one page. And he was carrying not just a major plot point—that Marvin and Casey were fighting over something—but also patterns he had noticed—that Marvin *keeps* saying, *"I don't care,"* *keeps* saying it after Stuart says it, and *keeps* saying, *"I bet she'll talk."* The word *keep* that Alex used indicates that he is noticing something that recurs or repeats. Readers who notice patterns and put them together in order to build meaning are readers who read complexly (Barnhouse and Vinton 2012). And because none of that information is conveyed explicitly on the page, I considered this text to be relatively complex for a reader like Alex.

Even though I could have asked Alex more questions—about what Marvin did that he feels bad about or why he keeps saying, *"I don't care"*—I thought I had seen enough of his thinking that I could do a notice-and-name conference.

DB: Alex, you're doing amazing thinking in this book. You're understanding that the author is having the character say the exact opposite of what he really feels! Do you know how tricky that is?

And do you know how you were able to do that? You noticed a pattern: you noticed on all these other pages that Marvin keeps saying, *"I don't care"* and that he only says it after his friend says it.

Noticing that pattern helped you understand that the author was showing something, which you think is that Marvin really does care.

I ended the conference by congratulating Alex and telling him to keep noticing patterns as he reads because those patterns will help him understand why characters are doing or saying what they are. He walked away beaming, which caused his teacher to comment, "He doesn't usually feel good about his reading." I could understand. How many students sit in our classrooms thinking that reading is saying the words perfectly? In our efforts to teach fluency, perhaps we have failed to remember that fluency and comprehension are not perfectly aligned. Ken and Yetta Goodman's work on miscue analysis has made a strong case for this. Reading, they say, needs to be both effective and efficient—effective in that the print has to make sense, and efficient in that readers need to expend the least amount of effort in order to make it make sense. Effective readers often make accurate meaning without slowing themselves down to get every word right (Goodman 1996). Clearly Alex, who was noticing deeply in this text and using what he noticed to make meaning despite his struggles with fluency, was being both effective and efficient: he was understanding the unstated parts of the story without having to get every word right.

Next Steps: Making More of Patterns

Even though I have used Alex as an example of a student reading complexly in a complex text, there are still some logical next steps for him. Now that he has been introduced to the concept of patterns and how they can help him infer, he will need lots of practice noticing different kinds of patterns in different books—something the teacher and I decided would be best introduced to the whole class in a read-aloud or shared reading context (Barnhouse and Vinton 2012).

In the meantime, we plan some follow-up conferences with Alex: the teacher will confer with him as he finishes this Marvin Redpost book (probably the next day or the day after) to see where his thinking has gone. In particular, she will follow up on the patterns he has noticed and see if and how those patterns have evolved or changed and what meaning Alex might make of that.

She also plans to ask Alex some why questions around these patterns: perhaps why he thinks Marvin had to agree with his friend and if he gained or lost anything in the end because of that; perhaps why he thinks the author decided to plant that or other patterns in the book to begin with and what those patterns might show the reader about the characters, the problems they face and how those problems are solved. How Alex answers these questions should reveal something about how he is thinking—hopefully with continued complexity.

Since this book is one in a series, the teacher can also steer Alex toward other Marvin Redpost books and push his thinking about the use of patterns in a series. Does Marvin say the same thing to Stuart in other books? Does he exhibit similar behavior, either with Stuart or with other characters? Does he face similar problems and are they solved in similar or different ways? Do the characters change or stay the same in the series, and if so how and why?

All this practice will help Alex gain confidence about his comprehension in texts that require lots of inferring—in other words, complex texts. After a bit of practicing with awareness about patterns and inferring across pages, I am confident he can be boosted up a level or two, which will put him in alignment with where the Common Core State Standards have determined he needs to be in third grade.

Next Steps: Understanding Issues Around Fluency

In terms of Alex's fluency, it would be interesting to do a retrospective miscue analysis with him. This is work that enables students to better understand the nature of their miscues (Goodman 1991). Many miscues are what are known as "high-quality miscues," meaning they are "syntactically and semantically acceptable" (Goodman 2008, 5). Most of Alex's miscues seemed to fall into this category because his substitutions made sense in the context of the story. A student like Alex can better understand himself as a reader—and so can his teachers and parents—if he can see that he is paying attention to semantic clues, or those that help him comprehend, above graphophonic cues, or those that are letter/sound coordinated. Perhaps this work can help Alex "revalue" himself as a reader (Goodman 1991), growing to see that rather than being a "poor" reader, he is a "thinking" reader, a reader who is making lots of decisions as he reads, decisions about what to focus on so he can most efficiently build meaning.

Perhaps as Alex reads harder and harder books he will have to slow himself down a little. Perhaps he will find that as he skips over or substitutes words his comprehension falters. At that point, with his teacher, he will have to take a closer look at some of the decisions he's making as a reader: When does he need to slow down? What graphophonic cues does he need to focus on? Until then, though, what purpose does slowing down serve him? At this point it only undermines his ability to trust the decisions he is making that allow him to be an effective and efficient reader.

When we want students to sustain complex thinking in more complex texts, it's important that we help them see:

- the thinking they are already doing;
- what that thinking yields—meaning, engagement, involvement with the characters and plot;

- the importance of patterns in books and how noticing patterns can deepen comprehension, understanding, and engagement;
- the decisions they are making as they read and what those decisions allow them to accomplish.

Summary

In each of the instances discussed in this chapter—whether a student is reading simply in simple texts, complexly in simple texts, or complexly in complex texts—I'm attempting to extend a student's understanding about how texts work and the thinking readers do. In this way, I'm hoping not just to get students to read more complex texts but to help them read more complexly. I am not merely handing these students a more complex book, which usually results in simple thinking (see Chapter 6), but specifying what they are doing, which will help them read more complex books more complexly. As Marie Clay writes, this work "allows the partially familiar to become familiar and the new to become partially familiar in an ever-changing sequence" (Clay 1991, 328). I retain high expectations for all my students in a way that meets each of them where they are.

The method of teaching I choose to move students up the staircase of text complexity is rooted in noticing and naming. This allows each student to be an agent in their own meaning making, becoming aware of how they are problem solving as they read and what that problem solving allows them to do in texts.

TOOLBOX ▶ FOLLOWING UP AND KEEPING TRACK

Check-in Conferences

In this chapter, I referred to check-in conferences with several of the students. These are quick conferences designed to follow up on work done during a previous research conference. Sometimes I don't even sit down during these conferences, but simply lean over a student as the class is first getting settled into independent reading or as the period is coming to a close.

I do check-in conferences with students to:

- make sure the student understands or is continuing to do the work we previously noticed and named together;
- give them a Book/Brain chart from work done in a previous conference;

- add on to a Book/Brain chart we've previously created;
- touch base about book choice or what page the student is on.

Using Conferences for Whole-Class Teaching

Conferences feed my whole-class teaching and vice versa. I'll often have a conference that I know will perfectly illustrate the thinking I want all students to be doing. I will frequently turn these conferences into mini-lessons for the whole class. Either during the share time or the mini-lesson time on a subsequent day, I will "retell" a powerful conference for the benefit of the whole class, perhaps charting some of the thinking the student did or showing a Book/Brain chart already created for an individual student. My conferences with Carlos and Alex in this chapter are examples of such work. These students were doing some big thinking—connecting ideas across pages and noticing patterns—that is applicable to any text. Unpacking such conferences with the whole class allows students to serve as the models for instruction, which feeds their agency.

Using Whole-Class Teaching in Conferences

Likewise, I often use my whole-class teaching to inform my conferences. I like to use the whole-class read-aloud or shared reading to make the big work of reading visible to all students. Inferring by connecting details across pages, getting into the habit of asking and answering *why* questions, and looking deeply at patterns are three such examples mentioned in this chapter. This is work that can't necessarily be captured in one or two mini-lessons but is best understood as students delve into pages and chapters over time in a book. As I then confer with students in their independent reading books, I will often make reference to the thinking we have done as a whole class. Students may, for example, be noticing patterns in a read-aloud; I can then follow up with individual students as I confer with them, asking what, if any, patterns they may be noticing in a book they are reading independently. Similarly, before I make individual Book/Brain charts for students, I will often have first introduced the concept and format during a whole-class reading experience so it will already be familiar to the students (see also Chapter 3).

Some Notes on Note Taking

One of the most frequently asked questions I get from teachers is about note taking. "Tell me how to take notes," they say. I used to think this was a straightforward question; if I told them how I take notes, they would replicate it and be happy. I was wrong. Note taking, it turns out, is a kind of window into our brains. Each of us has a different style. I will describe mine here, but know that it is personal and, to some, might appear to be a little quirky. There is no need to follow my style. What *is* necessary to follow, I think, are the purposes for note taking:

- to keep track of when we confer with whom;
- to capture the details and essence of what students say since this will inform our noticing-and-naming instruction;
- to hold ourselves accountable for our students' learning, keeping track of where they have been and what their instructional next steps might be;
- to hold our students accountable for what they're reading and what they're learning;
- to provide formative data for each of our students for use by us, by parents, and by administrators.

Taking Notes on Individual Students

Before the conference: I make sure that I have looked over any previous conference notes I might have on this student to remind myself what the student has been working on. While I have traditionally kept notes on a clipboard filled with blank pieces of paper, I am currently in the process of learning how to take notes electronically using the program Evernote (evernote.com). Cathy Mere, in her wonderful blog, *Reflect & Refine: Building a Learning Community* (2013), has been instrumental both in converting me to electronic note taking and in helping me realize the possibilities and benefits of this technology.

In any case, no matter what form you're working in, electronic or paper, you'll want to make sure you take down the name of the student, the date of the conference, the title of the book, and the page number the student is reading. Evernote allows you to also record the conference and/or to photograph the page the student is reading.

During the conference: Sometimes as students read I jot down words they are substituting or missing completely, but I don't usually do formal running records. I am more interested in talking to them about how they are problem solving as they read. I therefore try to get down some of the specific words students say or bring up as we talk. I am especially on the lookout for thinking words such as *maybe* or *I think* or *I'm not sure yet.*

After the conference: I take a few seconds to jot down any details I may have missed during the conference as well as some of my reflections. I usually put this information in the margins of my notes so I can refer back to it more easily. Sometimes I am able to immediately organize what I notice in a Book/Brain format in which case I make note of that.

Figure 4.7 is a sample of notes I took from a conference I had with a sixth grader, Veronica.

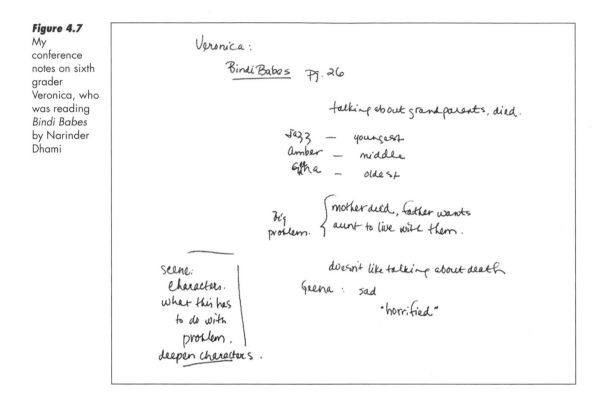

You can see that Veronica was reading page 26 of *Bindi Babes*, in which three sisters, Jazz, Amber, and Geena, are talking about an aunt coming to live with them because their grandparents and their mother are dead. Veronica has identified the characters, a few facts about them ("the youngest, middle, and oldest") and the "big problem" in the story. Additionally, Veronica says the girls don't really like talking about death. In response to my question about how she knew this, she pointed to the word *horrified*. In summary she thinks Geena and her sisters are feeling "sad."

The notes I made to myself after the conference appear in the left-hand margin. You can see that although I thought Veronica was holding on to the big problem and the characters, some next steps for her were to attend to details in each scene in order to consider how those details might be contributing to, complicating, or illuminating the big problem she has identified ("what this has to do with the big problem"). Additionally, I thought she could do some deeper work around the characters.

Over the years, mostly in response to teachers' requests, I have tried to organize my thinking into a template that teachers can use in their own classrooms. Figure 4.8 (and Appendix 4) is the effort that best represents the thinking I try to capture as I confer.

Figure 4.8 A note-taking chart filled in with notes from a sixth-grade class

Student Name, Date, Book Title, Page No.	What Student Says and Does	Textual Clues Student Uses	Possible Next Steps
Veronica 1/10 *Bindi Babes,* pg. 26	characters, main facts, big problem "sad"	"horrified"	how details connect to problem
Michael 2/4 *Diary of a Wimpy Kid,* pg. 203	character feeling "bad"	dialogue	more complex texts
Alyssa 2/11 *Boy in Striped PJs,* pg. 126	page-to-page inferring	"obvious"	inferring through patterns

Taking Notes on the Whole Class

As important as it is to keep track of individual conferences, it's equally important to keep track of conferences for the whole class, so at a glance I can see
whom I need to confer with. For this purpose, I rely on the tried-and-true method
used by many teachers: a simple template with the names of students running
down the left side and blank boxes filling the rest of the page. I put the date of
each conference in a box next to the student's name. Figure 4.9 is a sample.
Many teachers using electronic tablets find this format convenient and at the
touch of a screen move easily from whole-class notes to individual to small-
group notes. At a glance I can see who I need to confer with, who I need to do
a check-in conference with, and who is slated to be in a small group (see
Chapter 5).

Figure 4.9 Keeping track of students in a whole class (C/I denotes a check-in conference)

D'Andre	1/8	1/10 (C/I)	2/4															
Velma	2/4	2/21	3/7															
Chantal	1/8	1/28	3/8															
Teayana	1/8	2/12	3/8															
Michael	2/4	3/7	3/8 (C/I)															
Miguel	1/16	2/11																
Terrance	1/16	1/17 (C/I)																
Claire	1/28	1/29 (C/I)																
Alyssa	1/28	2/11																

No matter what format you use, notes should be easy to use and refer to.
Look over your notes before you have your next conference with a student or
before you plan a small group. Additionally, use your notes to help you pull
data together before parent-teacher conferences or in response to administrators who may want to see how you are keeping track of and using formative
data about your students.

CHAPTER

TEACHING SMARTER
Stepping Students Up to Do More Complex Thinking in Small Groups

My thoughts are stars I cannot fathom into constellations.

—John Green

Some years back I was working with a seventh-grade teacher who voiced a concern: some of her students who were doing great thinking in read-aloud were not doing the same kinds of work in their independent books.

"They have amazing ideas when I read to them," she said, "They interpret, they get themes, they're completely in the text, they do everything! But in their independent reading books? Nothing."

Was this about engagement? Book level? The inability to focus independently for thirty minutes without being distracted by one seventh-grade issue or another?

93

We hunkered down to do research conferences. It didn't take long to realize that most of the students the teacher was talking about were missing all kinds of textual clues as they read independently. It wasn't that they couldn't decode per se, although a few students did stumble over longer words and read through punctuation. Rather, they seemed to be reading the words without picking up on the meaning those words were pointing to, often meaning that was fundamental to the story, such as who was doing what, who was talking, or where the characters were.

When the teacher and I met after class to talk about our findings, we hypothesized that the kinds of clues these students were missing in their independent reading were the kinds of clues that the teacher was most likely providing support for during the read-aloud. The students could follow the clues when the story was read to them because the teacher's voice conveyed that information. However, when it came time to read on their own, they did not recognize the print cues that "told" the teacher to alter her voice.

The teacher thought perhaps it would help students to see what she was reading as she read aloud, so they could correlate the print cues with her voice. "Can I do shared reading with students who are this age?" she wondered. It seemed a worthwhile place to start, and so we made an effort to project the read-aloud text and to emphasize *how* readers knew what they knew in a text, not just *what* they knew.

And we continued doing research conferences during independent reading. We saw these same students often reading fluently but having trouble keeping track of characters; we saw that some had no idea what was going in dialogue that was written without attribution; we saw others relying on the back jacket to talk about some of the big ideas or themes in fiction, or relying on titles, subtitles, and pictures in nonfiction. Sure enough, many of these same students raised their hands eagerly during the whole-class work, sharing complex ideas and showing deep understanding.

I have never forgotten that class or that teacher's insights into her students' needs. Certainly, making sure that students' eyes are on the print as we read aloud is extremely helpful for students to correlate complex print cues with meaning. But I now think that's just a start. Many students have never received instruction around some of the mechanical aspects of texts that are essential for comprehension—how dialogue works, for example, or word clues that indicate time shifts. If they have had the benefit of looking closely at how texts work, it is usually done in the service of writing, with lessons emphasizing craft rather than comprehension.

Perhaps this is because the teaching we have tended to do around reading emphasizes *what* a student comprehends so much more than *how* they comprehend—a habit exacerbated by many of the instructional materials that are published in the name of the Common Core State Standards. These materials emphasize specific answers to specific prompts or "text-dependent" questions that the teacher is supposed to ask (Fisher and Frey 2012). Some prepared materials, such as those published by Pearson (2014), whose program is widely used in New York City, suggest that teachers form small groups based on the students who do not get specific answers to these questions. Essentially the groups are renewed attempts to help students "get" the "it" of the provided texts. There is no emphasis in these lessons on how readers know what they know in texts—only on what they know.

Emphasizing *what* over *how* in our instruction means we have often failed to pay attention to what research conferences reveal—namely, that students at every level need instruction to make visible the way texts work and the thinking that readers do as a result. It also means that we are focusing our teaching generally on complexity rather than specifically on the textual clues that make some texts more complex than others. We may do so because we assume that, as students move up levels in their independent reading, they must be capable of comprehending more complex print cues. Or we may assume that if students seem to be comprehending the whole-class text determined to be grade-level-appropriate in terms of text complexity, then we don't need to include any hows in our teaching.

If we are to move students up the staircase of text complexity—by which I mean if we are to move students to do more complex thinking in more complex texts—we need to make sure that students can navigate complex clues that will help them do complex thinking more independently. We therefore need to make sure we teach smarter by:

- emphasizing *how* readers know what they know in texts;
- moving beyond the labels that have been given to texts (Lexiles, levels, or grade-level complexity) and grounding our teaching in more specificity;
- maintaining each student's role as problem solver.

Stepped-Up Small Groups

If I could return to that seventh-grade class whose students are probably well into adulthood by now, I would add to the teacher's toolbox. In addition to doing more shared reading with those students who struggled to make sense of print, I would try some stepped-up small-group lessons. I first wrote about stepped-up instruction in *What Readers Really Do* (Barnhouse and Vinton 2012). *Readers Front & Center* delves more deeply into the concept and explores some of the how-tos involved.

As you are no doubt aware, some readers, in the words of Marie Clay, are "effective" and some are not. Those who are effective have developed what Clay calls a "self-extending system of literacy expertise," meaning that as they read "they are able to notice new things about words or print or messages, constructively linking these to other things they know" (Clay 1991, 319). In other words, they learn to read by reading.

These students have figured out—through reading—the clues that go into helping them construct an understanding of what they are reading. They understand how print works, how words and sentences are built; they figure out tricky time clues, dialogue, and pronouns; they realize when they are getting information directly as well as indirectly. And they seem to "just know" these things, usually reading without consciousness about how they know what they know. These readers seem to progress just by virtue of the fact that they are reading. They truly appear to be reading from inside the text.

And then there are the readers who aren't effective. Stepped-up small-group lessons are an attempt to help these "low progress readers" (Clay 1991) learn to read by reading. By being shown *how* readers know what they know, these readers can be made aware of textual clues that will help them develop systems of "literacy expertise" and enable them to become more self-extending as they construct meaning in texts. In other words, they will be able to read more independently and to read increasingly complex texts.

Stepped-up lessons are designed to increase a reader's awareness of textual clues by starting out with texts that have clear and sometimes obvious clues and ending with those that have less explicit or complex clues. Since *explicit* is a relative word—what is explicit for one reader may be implicit for another—this is work that not everyone in a class typically needs. I therefore prefer teaching stepped-up lessons around print cues to small groups of students. Some examples of stepped-up lessons appropriate for whole-class work appear in Chapter 6.

I plan stepped-up small groups from two angles—the students and the texts. In addition, I always emphasize the process of reading.

Planning from What Students Need

Research conferences allow me to burrow into pages alongside students and observe them as they problem-solve. After conferences with many, if not all, of the students in a class, I begin to recognize patterns emerging among the readers.

In a fifth-grade class, for example, I noticed several patterns from my conferences: some students were losing track of their comprehension when they were confronted with longer, more complex sentences; a few students became confused by subtle time clues that shifted the scene; and dialogue proved tricky for some—both following who was saying what and recognizing specific information being conveyed indirectly through the characters' speech.

A chart of some of the patterns I noticed from this class and some ideas about possible small-group stepped-up lessons appears in Figure 5.1 (see Appendix 5 for a chart template).

Much of what I put on this chart is what students are not doing well. You may wonder how this fits with the philosophy I've been advocating about

Figure 5.1 Patterns I notice from my conferences in a fifth-grade class

Patterns From Conferences	Possible Stepped-Up Teaching Points
Raoul—loses track in complex sentences Michelle—not sure who is doing what in longer sentences Benny—follows action but not longer passages of description Eliza—Not sure who is in scene	Complex sentences (buried subject)
Cooper—not always keeping track of scene; not sure where character is Marcos—loses scene Royce—loses action when buried in longer passages Michelle—loses scene in flashback	Flashbacks/time cues Or Background info versus present scene Or Getting information in indirect ways
Kaitlyn—pronouns in dialogue seem tricky Marcos—unattributed dialogue Trevor—skipping dialogue?	Dialogue
Raoul—not sure of name of 'I' narrator Marcos—not thinking back as he gets more info Angelica—skipping over description	Point of view Or Getting information in indirect ways

starting instruction from what students are doing well. It's important to remember that I have done at least one research conference with each of these students, during which I have noticed and named something they are doing well and something they know about how texts work. In some cases, additional conferences extended the students into more complex thinking and more complex texts, as described in Chapter 4. Keeping these small groups framed around problem solving helps me continually emphasize that it's the texts that are problems, not the students.

Unlike traditional guided reading groups, these small groups are not necessarily formed according to students' reading levels. I could, for example, have students in one group reading in a range of levels between, say, L and O or J and M. This is because the focus of a stepped-up group is relatively narrow and heavily scaffolded: I use a small section of a text rather than the whole book, and I often read the texts I'm using out loud to take care of any fluency or pacing issues that might arise due to the varying levels.

Planning from Texts

In addition to planning stepped-up lessons from the conferences I have with students, I also plan based on what I notice in the texts that students typically read. This is not the same as choosing a text based on its level. I often don't look at the levels of texts I work with in small groups. As mentioned in Chapter 1, levels are labels and, though labels can be useful as assessments, they are not usually useful as instructional tools. Moving a student up the level ladder is not the same as teaching that student. I need to frame my instruction in these groups around specific ways that texts work and specific thinking that those texts require; levels do not allow for such specificity—and can often obscure it.

What I do instead of relying on the level of a book is look closely at actual texts. If I don't have time to read the whole book, I open up the first pages and read them, then thumb through some middle pages and read a few paragraphs. As I read, I'm asking myself what I know and how I know it (Figure 5.2 and Appendix 1), a way of thinking about texts introduced in the Toolbox in Chapter 2. This helps me see what is explicitly revealed on the page and what is implicitly revealed.

As an example, look at the opening of *Tales of a Fourth Grade Nothing* by Judy Blume.

> *I won Dribble at Jimmy Fargo's birthday party. All the other guys got to take home goldfish in little plastic bags. I won him because I guessed*

Figure 5.2 Using the What I Know/How I Know It chart to help plan small groups

What I Know (from the text)	How I Know It

> *there were three hundred and forty-eight jelly beans in Mrs. Fargo's jar. Really, there were four hundred and twenty-three, she told us later. Still, my guess was closest. "Peter Warren Hatcher is the big winner!" Mrs. Fargo announced.*
>
> *At first I felt bad that I didn't get a goldfish too. Then Jimmy handed me a glass bowl. Inside there was some water and three rocks. A tiny green turtle was sleeping on the biggest rock. All the other guys looked at their goldfish. I knew what they were thinking. They wished they could have tiny green turtles too.*
>
> *I named my turtle Dribble while I was walking home from Jimmy's party.* (Blume 1972, 3–4)

At first glance this seems like a pretty straightforward piece. In thinking about what I know, I know who the character is, where he is, what he's doing, and how he's feeling. But when I look at *how* I know what I know, I see all kinds of potentially tricky things (Figure 5.3). I see that the name of the "I" narrator is revealed indirectly, through dialogue; I see that the reader is introduced to Dribble before we find out that it is a "him" (in the third

Figure 5.3 A What I Know/How I Know It chart filled in from the opening paragraph of *Tales of a Fourth Grade Nothing*

What I Know (from the text)	How I Know It
The character's name is Peter Warren Hatcher	Implied through dialogue ["Peter Warren Hatcher is the big winner!" Mrs. Fargo announced]
Dribble is a turtle	Implied through action [Jimmy hands him a bowl with a turtle inside it] Stated in third paragraph [I named my turtle Dribble while I was walking home . . .]
Opening paragraphs are a flashback	Stated time clues [later, at first, then, while] Implied time clues [because]

sentence) and before we find out he is a turtle, which is implied in the second paragraph but not explicitly stated until the third paragraph (*I named my turtle Dribble while I was walking home from Jimmy's party.*). That sentence also tells me that the opening two paragraphs have been a flashback, which makes me notice some of the other time clues at play here—some very clear (*at first, then, later*) and some more implied (*because*).

Any of these how-we-know-what-we-know issues could be potential teaching points, and since each of them can be placed on a continuum of implicit to explicit or simple to complex, each can be a possible lesson that can be taught using the stepped-up method.

For some students the passage from *Tales of a Fourth Grade Nothing* might be difficult since it's not told in chronological time and has an indirect time clue, *because*, that implies one event preceding another. For these students, this text might be the last step in a series that starts with simpler time clues, perhaps a text such as *Mr. Putter and Tabby See the Stars* by Cynthia Rylant (2007), which contains several flashbacks but uses explicit time clues (*tonight, before he, Then when, In the morning*) and does so with picture support (pictures of Mr. Putter as a boy while the words say, *He told her about looking at stars when he was a boy*, and pictures of him in his pajamas juxtaposed with pictures of him in day clothes). Or a simpler text might be *Diary of a Wimpy Kid* (Kinney 2010), which combines a present-tense narrative with flashbacks that are told in a simple past tense and supported by explicit

Figure 5.4 Examples of stepped-up texts from simple to more complex time clues

		Frequent flashbacks with explicit and implied clues (*because*)
	Occasional use of flashbacks Explicit time clues (*before, then, on Monday*) Picture support Past perfect tense	
Straight chronological time frame		
Examples: *Stink: The Incredible Shrinking Kid* *Ready Freddy! Tooth Trouble*	Examples: *Mr. Putter and Tabby* *Diary of a Wimpy Kid* *Clementine*	Example: *Tales of a Fourth Grade Nothing*

textual clues (*last spring, then one day*) or *Clementine* by Sara Pennypacker (2006), which use clear time clues (*Monday, first*). An even simpler first step would be choosing a section from one of the many books that are told in a straight chronological time frame without any use of flashbacks. The Ready Freddy! books by Abby Klein or the Stink books by Megan McDonald are all such examples (Figure 5.4).

For other students, the time clues in *Tales of a Fourth Grade Nothing* might be very clear (*at first* and *then*). This, then, could be the first text in a series that stepped into something more complex, perhaps like the opening of *The Tiger Rising*, which uses a few straightforward time clues (*after, that's when*) but also the past perfect tense (*had been*) to indicate a flashback, which may be unfamiliar to or tricky for some students.

That morning, after he discovered the tiger, Rob went and stood under the Kentucky Star Motel sign and waited for the school bus just like it was any other day. The Kentucky Star sign was composed of a yellow neon star that rose and fell over a piece of blue neon in the shape of the state of Kentucky. Rob liked the sign; he harbored a dim but abiding notion that it would bring him luck.

Finding the tiger had been luck, he knew that. He had been out in the woods, not really looking for anything, just wandering, hoping that maybe he would get lost or get eaten by a bear and not have to go to school ever again. That's when he saw the old Beauchamp gas station building, all boarded up and tumbling down; next to it, there was a cage, and inside the cage, unbelievably, there was a tiger—a real life, very large tiger pacing back and forth. (DiCamillo 2006, 1–2)

Next steps up from *Tiger Rising* might be a text that uses just a light sprinkle of past perfect to convey something that occurred in a "prior past" point in time. Jerry Spinelli employs this tense in *The Library Card (Weasel had said)*. That one little word *had* is easy to miss. An inexperienced reader could very well gloss over it and believe, mistakenly it turns out, that Weasel is in the store with Mongoose.

Fingers trembling, eyes on the man at the cash register, Mongoose snatched the Milky Way bar and stuck it in his coat pocket.

He waited for lightning to strike. For the hand of God to frizzle him on the spot. The earth to open and swallow him up. Cops at least.

Nothing.

Nothing but himself standing in front of the candy section of the Mini-Mart feeling like a dope. He couldn't believe he was fooling anybody.

"Look like you're checking the stuff out," Weasel had said. "Like you're tryin' to decide what to buy."

Right. So here he was, scratching the back of his head and putting this stupid now-what-do-I-want-to-buy-look on his face. Meanwhile stuffing a candy bar into his pocket. (Spinelli 1997, 3)

There are many more complex texts that don't use signal words at all but simply jump, movielike, from one scene to another. *Sarah, Plain and Tall*, the Common Core exemplar text for second and third graders (see Chapter 4), uses this technique.

Caleb thought the story was over, and I didn't tell him what I had really thought. He was homely and plain, and he had a terrible holler and a horrid smell. But these were not the worst of him. Mama died the next morning. That was the worst thing about Caleb.

"Isn't he beautiful, Anna?" Her last words to me. I had gone to bed thinking how wretched he looked. And I forgot to say good night.

I wiped my hands on my apron and went to the window. Outside, the prairie reached out and touched the places where the sky came down. Though winter was nearly over, there were patches of snow and ice everywhere. I looked at the long dirt road that crawled across the plains, remembering the morning that Mama had died, cruel and sunny. (MacLachlan 1985, 5)

There are a few references to time (*the next morning* in the first paragraph and *remembering the morning that Mama died* in the last paragraph) and the use of the past perfect tense, but mostly no direct clues that the scenes are changing. Instead, there is a "present moment" or scene that has been established and then changes. In this case, the scene that has been established is one in which Caleb and the narrator (Anna) are talking in the kitchen. The flashback scene is one in which Anna is with her mother during Caleb's birth. There is then a return to an action that dovetails with the original scene (*I wiped my hands on my apron*) and also some additional references to the original setting (*the window* and *winter*). These types of signals require a reader to hold on to information across paragraphs and pages and actively make within-text connections. Figure 5.5 shows a possible stepped-up series regarding these more complex time clues.

Figure 5.5 Examples of stepped-up texts with more complex time clues

Frequent flashbacks with explicit and implied clues (*because*)	Flashbacks interwoven into narrative, signaled only with use of past perfect tense Occasional explicit time clues	Light use of past perfect tense Use of scene changes to indicate change in time	Few if any direct time clues Use of scene changes to indicate change in time
Example: *Tales of a Fourth Grade Nothing*	Example: *Tiger Rising*	Example: *The Library Card*	Example: *Sarah, Plain and Tall*

The Process of Reading

In addition to planning small groups from the texts students are reading and from the students I teach, I always want to make sure I am emphasizing the process of reading. This helps students understand that they can—and should—always be problem solvers as they read. So even as I organize a lesson around nitty-gritty textual clues, I want to make sure students are able to see and experience how readers hold on to confusion or *not knowing* something and read forward expecting clarity (Barnhouse and Vinton 2012).

Simpler texts, in general, provide information more directly and therefore result in less confusion for a reader. For example, the opening sentence of *Tales of a Fourth Grade Nothing*—*I won Dribble at Jimmy Fargo's birthday party*—begs the question, Who is Dribble? A simpler text might be phrased something like this: *I won a turtle at Jimmy Fargo's birthday party and named him Dribble on my way home.* The reader of the latter sentence certainly reads on with general questions—Who is this "I" narrator and who is Jimmy Fargo and how is this information going to add up?—but not the specific question about who Dribble is. That information has been directly stated. A slightly more complex phrasing might be something like this: *I won Dribble at Jimmy Fargo's birthday party. Dribble is a turtle.* This first sentence still begs the question, Who is Dribble?, but the answer is provided almost immediately.

A reader of a more complex text needs a fair amount of stamina to gather and connect multiple clues and also needs an understanding that this is the way texts are designed. Language, both written and oral, has what is known as "redundancy" (Smith 2004), meaning that information is provided not by one but by multiple clues. A reader comprehends by checking and cross-checking textual clues. Because this is an active process, confusion and revision are at the heart of how we read (Barnhouse and Vinton 2012). I may, then, approach the passage in *Sarah, Plain and Tall*, for example, initially thinking that the mother is in the kitchen with Caleb and Anna. But as I keep reading I collect more clues and think back to what I've already read, clarifying clues I've retained, and in that way, I correct or adjust my understanding.

Through this process of clarification, I am adding on to my understanding of how texts work and the thinking I have to do in order to comprehend as I read. This process, as mentioned in Chapter 4, "allows the partially familiar to become familiar and the new to become partially familiar in an ever-changing sequence" (Clay 1991, 328). It allows the text to teach the reader. This is ultimately where we want all our students to be so they can truly read more independently and proficiently. If I teach students to follow textual clues without simultaneously making visible the process of moving from confusion to clarity, I will be missing an opportunity to show these students how to become "high-progress" readers who can learn to read by reading.

Putting Texts and Students Together to Plan

By getting in the habit of looking at texts with an eye toward what you know and how you know it, you'll be aware of possible next steps for your students. By conferring with your students and noticing patterns in your classroom, you will be aware of who needs what and when they may be ready for next steps. Let's now look at how we can bring our knowledge of texts and our knowledge of students together to teach a specific lesson.

First, I look over my conferring notes and patterns I see emerging from a class. In the fifth-grade class I introduced earlier, Michelle was reading a Beverly Cleary book, *Ramona the Brave*. In my research conference with her I had noticed that she was getting characters and scenes mixed up. Her comprehension seemed to particularly stall as she tried to wade through some of Cleary's long sentences, such as this one: *She was impatient because no matter how many times her mother telephoned, the workmen had not come to start the new room, and if they did not start the new room, how was Ramona going to astound the first grade by telling them about the hole chopped in the house?* (Cleary 1975, 45–46).

Eliza was reading *Rules* by Cynthia Lord when I conferred with her and seemed to have particular trouble following sentences that weren't long but had what I think of as "buried" subjects, sentences like this one—*Waiting for the song to finish, I run my thumb along an edge of my word cards* (Lord 2006, 68)—which was from a page she was reading when I first conferred with her, and this one—*Ryan waves, standing on the sand at the shore* (Lord 2006, 141)—which she was reading a few days later.

There are proper grammatical terms for the sentence constructions that Michelle and Eliza were encountering, and I briefly considered doing a small-group lesson about the grammar of such sentences, but then I conferred with Benny and Raoul, who were both reading books in the Percy Jackson series by Rick Riordan. These books don't have long sentences per se but do have complicated paragraphs with many twists and distractions, as exemplified by this section that Benny was reading:

The walls were hung with animal pelts: black bear, tiger, and several others I didn't recognize. I figured an animal rights activist would've had a heart attack looking at all those rare skins, but maybe since Artemis was the goddess of the hunt, she could replenish whatever she shot. I thought she had another animal pelt lying next to her, and then I realized it was a live animal—a deer with glittering fur and silver horns, its head resting contentedly in Artemis's lap. (Riordan 2008, 38)

As I thought about patterns emerging from my conferences (see Figure 5.1), I began to see that the issues Benny and Raoul faced in their texts seemed similar to those that Eliza and Michelle were facing—namely, keeping track of who was doing what. I recognized that Eliza and Michelle's comprehension seemed to have less to do with grammar per se, meaning the terminology or label of how those sentences were constructed, and more to do with how a reader keeps track of texts that are written in convoluted, or complex, ways.

I like to keep my small groups to about four students. Three can work but five is often too many to give every student a chance to share and talk equally. Since time is always of the essence in classrooms, I like to plan groups that last no longer than twenty minutes. For this reason, I often only teach two or three texts in one stepped-up lesson. The more texts you teach, the more time you need. If you plan on taking three or more steps up with your students, which would require the use of three or more texts, consider splitting your lesson into two days (or spending the whole period with the group).

When I get in front of students with a few texts in my hand, I can drift. There's so much to talk about and the kids have such interesting insights. There is a time and place for interesting talk, but for stepped-up small-group lessons I like to be focused and planned. I therefore developed a template that helps me stay on task (see Appendix 6). Figure 5.6 shows this template filled in with the lesson I did with Raoul, Michelle, Benny, and Eliza.

I had three steps in mind, illustrated by three texts. I knew because of time constraints that the third text was an "on-deck" text that I might or might not have time for or that the students might not yet be ready for.

Conducting the Lesson

While the rest of the class was doing independent reading, I gathered these four students together at a table in the back of the classroom and explained what we were going to work on together and why I had chosen them for this group. I always try to start my small-group lessons with something positive I noticed the students doing in my conferences with them:

DB: When I last saw each of you, I noticed some great reading work you were doing. Benny and Raoul, you guys were keeping track of these

Figure 5.6 Planning a stepped-up small-group lesson on sentence complexity for fifth graders

Teaching point for today's group: How to follow complex sentences/passages

How this helps with reading: Helps readers keep track of who is doing what in order to follow complex stories more accurately

Resources (Texts to Use):

Step 1: *Stink*

Step 2: *Because of Winn-Dixie*

Step 3: *Bud, Not Buddy*

What I'll say/ask (How-can-we-figure-out questions):

How can we figure out what's going on in complex sentences that have lots of parts?
What information do sentences give readers?
What's going on in these sentences?
How can we break long sentences into parts, thinking about who is doing what?

What I'll look for:

Step 1: Understanding of who is doing what
Understanding of other sentences that aren't only about characters and action

Step 2: Understanding of two characters in one sentence doing different things
Understanding difference between someone doing something and someone who is having something done to them

Step 3: Applying understanding to a paragraph

Assessment/Application/Follow-up:

Student Name	What the Student Does/Says	Possible Next Steps
Eliza		
Benny		
Raoul		
Michelle		

complicated plots filled with tons of characters doing all sorts of bizarre things. And Eliza and Michelle, you were both really immersed in the characters in the books you were reading.

Today, we're going to work on a strategy to help you get even closer to characters as you read more and more complicated books. When you get into harder books, lots of things are harder: there are more pages, there are more characters, the plots are more complicated—and sometimes the sentences get harder to follow.

Today we're going to focus on sentences. They can be longer, they can have lots of commas or semicolons, or there can be more than one thing going on in one sentence. We're going to look at how readers can figure out what's going on in complicated sentences and what information they give readers.

But before we look at really hard sentences, we're going to back up a little and look at some easier ones. This will help us see the skeleton, or basics, of a sentence a little more easily.

I write the focus question for this group on a piece of paper that they can all see (Figure 5.7). Appendix 7 contains a template for creating similar inquiry charts with students.

Figure 5.7
The inquiry question for a small-group lesson on complex sentences

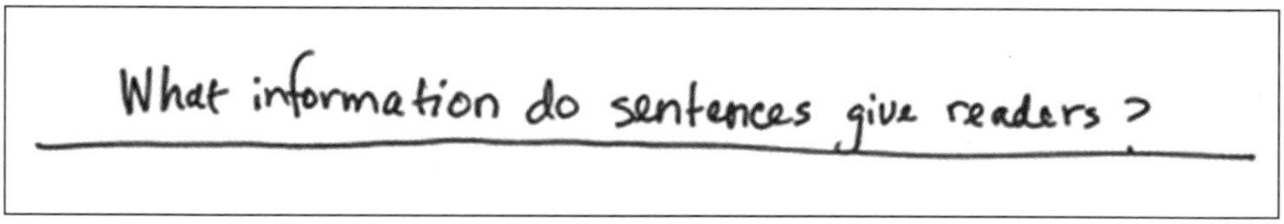

What information do sentences give readers?

I passed out a photocopied page from Chapter 2 of *Stink: The Incredible Shrinking Kid* by Megan McDonald, said a few words to introduce the story ("It's about a boy named Stink who is sick of being short and is afraid he's shrinking"), and read it out loud:

> *When Stink woke up the next morning, his bed felt as big as a country. The ceiling was up there with the sky. And it was a long way down to the floor. When he went to brush his teeth, even the sink seemed too tall.* (McDonald 2005, 13)

DB: So what are some things that are going on in these sentences, what are they telling us?

Raoul: Stink thinks his bed is as big as a country.

DB: Show us where you got that information. [Points to the phrase.] Yup. What else?

Benny: He brushes his teeth. [Reads the phrase.]
DB: Anything else?
Eliza: He wakes up in the morning.
DB: Great. So you guys all noticed the sentences that told the reader who the character was and what he was doing. [Writes *Who the Character Is* and *What They're Doing* on the paper.]

You will notice that as the students cite specific textual clues, I write down a generalization in an attempt to make their thinking applicable to more than one text.

DB: But there are other sentences here too, right? Let's look at those sentences. What's going on in those sentences? Michelle?

I called on Michelle because she had not yet volunteered information. I like to make sure all students are participating equally and sometimes find I need to call on students in small groups if they're not volunteering.

Michelle: *The ceiling was up there with the sky.*
DB: Yeah. So, what is that sentence telling you, Michelle?
Michelle: That the ceiling is high.
DB: So, is that sentence telling us about a character and what they're doing or do we need to add on to our list about what sentences do?
Benny: It's like describing the ceiling.
DB: Interesting.

In my planning, I had not thought of this sentence as description so much as recognized that it was different from those sentences that conveyed the main action of the narrative. My "look-for" (see Figure 5.6), therefore, had not been about the labels I expected students to provide so much as it was about their understanding. Not every student would label this as description; it could also be thought of as "what the character is thinking" or "how the character is feeling." I decided to echo the word Benny used because it exhibited the understanding I was expecting so I added that thinking to the chart (Figure 5.8).

DB: Are there any other sentences in this section that are describing something?
Benny: [Reads.] *And it was a long way down to the floor.*
DB: What's that describing?

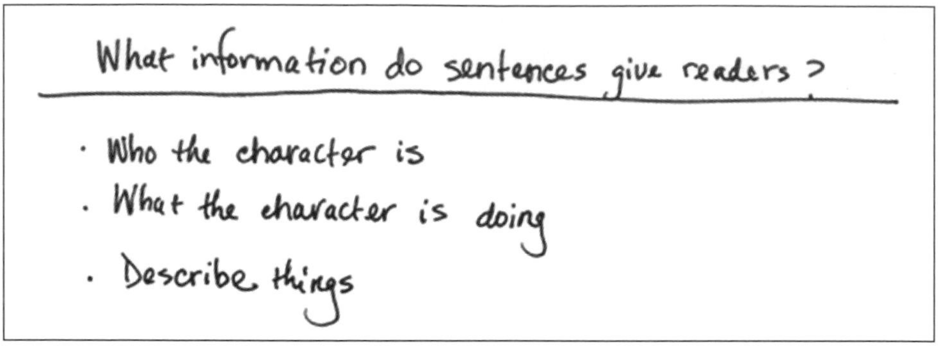

Figure 5.8
Generalizing
students'
answers to the
inquiry
question

> What information do sentences give readers?
>
> - Who the character is
> - What the character is doing
> - Describe things

Eliza: His bed. It's a long way from the floor.

DB: OK. So, let's reread all these sentences to see if we're getting all the information. We have Stink doing things: waking up in the morning, thinking his bed is big, brushing his teeth. We also have a description of the ceiling and of the bed being so far from the floor. Any other information we're getting from these sentences? Raoul?

Raoul: The sink.

DB: Say more.

Raoul: *The sink seems too tall.*

Eliza: It's describing the sink.

DB: Ah, more description. So we've seen that some sentences tell readers who the characters are and what they're doing and some sentences describe things. And this sentence—*When he went to brush his teeth, even the sink seemed too tall*—does both: the beginning of the sentence tells what Stink was doing and the last part describes the sink. [Adds this to the chart; see Figure 5.9.] Now, let's take this thinking into a slightly harder text.

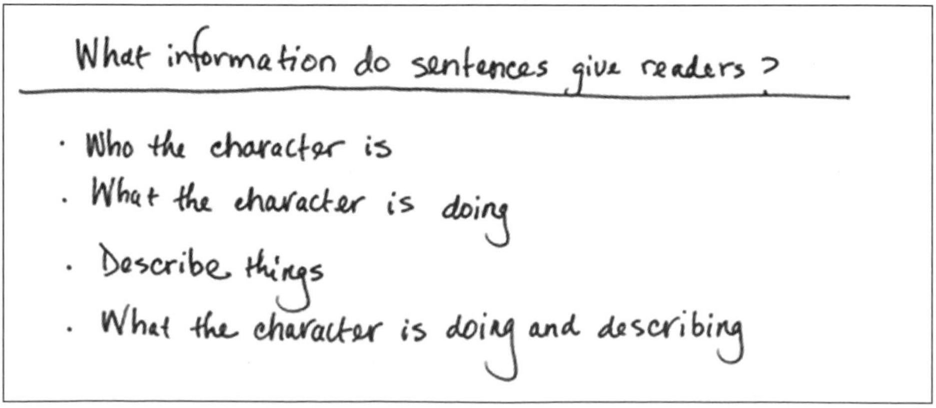

Figure 5.9
Adding on to
the inquiry
question as
students
explore more
sentences

> What information do sentences give readers?
>
> - Who the character is
> - What the character is doing
> - Describe things
> - What the character is doing and describing

I passed out a photocopy of the second text I was using—page 70 from *Because of Winn-Dixie* by Kate DiCamillo—and again gave some context for the excerpt, that this was a story narrated by a girl named Opal, who found a stray dog whom she named Winn-Dixie. I also explained that the preacher was her father, and then read the piece out loud:

> *That night when the preacher was tucking me into bed, I told him how I got a job at Gertrude's Pets, and I told him all about making friends with Miss Franny Block and getting invited to Sweetie Pie's party, and I told him about meeting Gloria Dump. Winn-Dixie lay on the floor, waiting for the preacher to leave so he could hop up on the bed like he always did. When I was done talking, the preacher kissed me good night, and then he leaned way over and gave Winn-Dixie a kiss, too, right on top of his head.*

DB: So, let's look at what we learned about sentences from *Stink*. [Points to the chart the group created.] They can tell readers about a character and about what that character is doing—and they can do all of that together.

So, how about these sentences from *Winn-Dixie*? Are these sentences doing the same things? Different things? Do we need to add anything to our list about what sentences tell a reader?

I gave students time to reread the text on their own. With other students I might choose to read it aloud a second time.

DB: Let's start with the first sentence.
Eliza: It's about a lot of different things.
DB: Yeah, it is. What's one thing it's about?
Eliza: The girl is telling the preacher about her job and about making friends with . . .
Raoul: Miss Franny Block.
Michelle: And about a party.
DB: OK, so that's maybe three things you noticed that this sentence is about.
Benny: It's all about her telling the preacher a lot of different things while he's tucking her into bed.
DB: Say more, Benny.
Benny: It says: *That night when the preacher was tucking me into bed, I told him . . .* and then she tells him all this stuff.

DB: Whoa, Benny, hold on. Are you saying that this sentence is telling us not just about what *one* character is doing but about what *another* character is doing too?

Benny: [Looks at the text.]

DB: What do you guys think?

Everyone: [Looks back at text.]

Raoul: Yeah. The first part is the preacher tucking her into bed and then she is telling the preacher about these things she's done.

DB: I'm going to add that to our list: sentences can tell us about what more than one character is doing [see Figure 5.10].

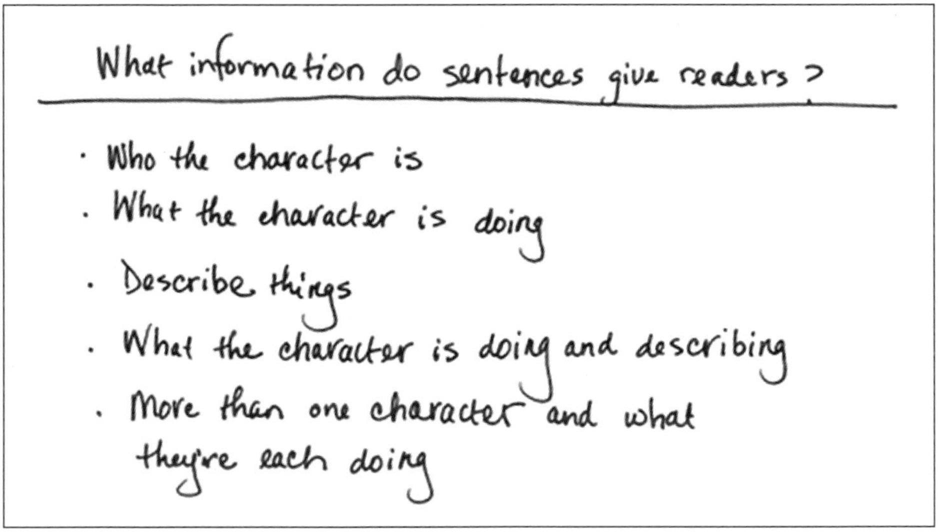

Figure 5.10
Adding to the inquiry question as students step up to more complex sentences

> What information do sentences give readers?
>
> · Who the character is
> · What the character is doing
> · Describe things
> · What the character is doing and describing
> · More than one character and what they're each doing

DB: Let's look at the second sentence. [Reads.] *Winn-Dixie lay on the floor, waiting for the preacher to leave so he could hop up on the bed like he always did.*

Benny: It's about one character.

DB: Who?

Benny: Winn-Dixie.

Michelle: But it has the preacher in it too.

DB: So, two characters? Let's look at what those characters are doing.

Raoul: Winn-Dixie is laying on the floor.

DB: And the preacher? Michelle?

Michelle: He's leaving.

DB: Show me how you know that.

Michelle: It says here, *waiting for the preacher to leave.*

Benny: But he hasn't left yet. He's getting ready to leave.

DB: How do you know that Benny?

Benny: It says, *waiting for the preacher to leave.*

DB: So who's doing the waiting in that sentence? Michelle?

Michelle: Um.

DB: Tricky, right? Let's read the sentence from the beginning to get the "who" back in our minds. [Reads.] *Winn-Dixie lay on the floor, waiting for the preacher to leave so he could hop up on the bed like he always did.*

Michelle: Oh, Winn-Dixie.

DB: Yeah. So this is what's tricky about sentences, right? This sentence mentions two characters just like the first sentence did, but only one of them is doing the action in this sentence.

Eliza: It's kind of like Winn-Dixie is thinking about the preacher leaving.

DB: Interesting. Let's add this to our list because it's a little more complicated [see Figure 5.11]. So this is a sentence where one character is doing more than one thing: he's lying on the floor and he's thinking and waiting.

Figure 5.11
Adding to the inquiry question as students continue to work with more complex sentences

What information do sentences give readers?

- Who the character is
- What the character is doing
- Describe things
- What the character is doing and describing
- More than one character and what they're each doing
- One character and more than one thing they're doing

DB: Let's read the final sentence and look at our list to see if we need to add anything to our chart. [Reads.] *When I was done talking, the preacher kissed me good night, and then he leaned way over and gave Winn-Dixie a kiss, too, right on top of his head.*

Benny: There are two characters.

Michelle: Three.

DB: Who?

Michelle: The girl, the preacher, and Winn-Dixie.

DB: OK, so again we have a sentence that's about more than one character. [Points to chart.] Now let's do what we did in the other sentences and look at what those characters are doing.

Raoul: The preacher is kissing her good night and then kisses Winn-Dixie.

DB: And how about the other characters—what are they doing?

Benny: Nothing.

DB: Nothing? You mean they're freeloading? Just hanging out? I could take them out of this sentence and everything would be fine?

Benny: No. The girl is done talking. And Winn-Dixie is getting kissed.

Eliza: It's like it's describing him getting kissed, *on top of his head.*

DB: Interesting thinking! Let's try to add that to our list [see Figure 5.12]. What you're saying is that only one character is doing something and that the other character, Winn-Dixie, isn't really doing something so much as having something done *to* him. Yes? And Eliza, you're saying that's a kind of description.

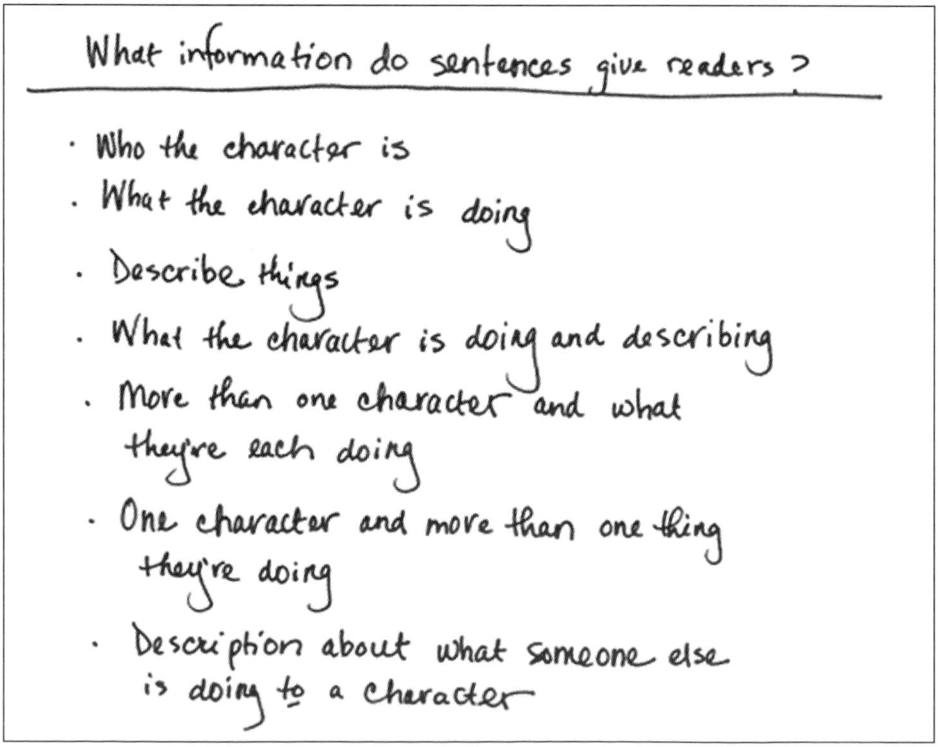

Figure 5.12
Reaching the final step in answer to the inquiry question

What information do sentences give readers?

- Who the character is
- What the character is doing
- Describe things
- What the character is doing and describing
- More than one character and what they're each doing
- One character and more than one thing they're doing
- Description about what someone else is doing to a character

I realized at this point that the two texts I had chosen had provided these students with plenty to think about and a lot to practice in their independent reading books. Pushing into the third step, a passage from *Bud, Not Buddy*, was going to be too much for one day. Instead, I summarized the thinking these students had done together:

DB: So, today we shined a spotlight on sentences and how they work. We saw that sentences give readers a lot of information and sometimes in tricky ways. To help you as you read tricky sentences, think about *who* is doing *what*.

We saw that sometimes sentences can have characters doing more than one thing or they can combine different characters doing different things and sometimes they can describe not what a character is doing but what someone else is doing *to* that character.

Keeping track of tricky sentences in this way will help you keep better track of the stories you're reading.

In debriefing this lesson with the classroom teacher, we decided that each student could benefit from receiving a copy of the notes I took. This would help remind them of what we had talked about and also help guide the teacher as she did check-in conferences during the rest of the week. Often the notes I take as students do stepped-up work can fit into a bookmark-shaped piece of paper that students keep with them as they read; at other times, as with this group, the thinking takes up a little more space, in which case the notes can be stapled or pasted into a student's reading notebook or folder for quick reference. Mostly, it's my hope that students will only need these notes for a short time, as a way to make visible some of the ways that complex texts work. As teachers, it's our goal to help students grow and develop an awareness that will help them eventually do this work automatically and independently.

Following Up

In addition to giving students a record of the work we did in the group, I keep my own records on each student. These records consist of brief jottings, taken during the group work, about what each student has said or done and, after the group is finished, possible next steps (Figure 5.13).

You can see that I was thinking that Eliza and Benny seemed ready to move on to more complex passages, based on some of the points they had

Figure 5.13 Keeping track of students during the group and considering next steps after the group

Assessment/Application/Follow-up:

Student Name	What the Student Does/Says	Possible Next Steps
Eliza	Character having something done to him is like "description" Following time clues	Ready for academic language about subject and object Ready for more complex passages
Benny	"Describing" Generalizing from one text to another	Ready for more complex passages A closer look at punctuation
Raoul	Following multiple actions, following time clues ("then")	More complex time clues
Michelle	Preacher leaving "Three characters"	More practice with who is doing the main action Build awareness of punctuation Push into time clues? (*during, while*)

made—in particular, their insight into how the more complex sentences "described." That Benny first noticed the way the sentences in *Stink* "described" and that Eliza built on it in *Because of Winn-Dixie* seemed to demonstrate an awareness of how sentences worked, which helped them generalize and transfer their thinking. Raoul and Michelle, on the other hand, seemed more tentative and less flexible, perhaps simply by way of habit. When Michelle was forced to slow down she followed the sentences but didn't seem to do so on her own. Raoul was not an active participant in the group, so it was hard to get a sense of how much he was comprehending on his own. I decided that both students would benefit from more practice in thinking about who is doing what in complex sentences or passages. A few check-in conferences about this work in their independent texts would help.

I was also thinking that the very clear time clues in *Because of Winn-Dixie* (*that night, when, then*) might have provided an additional support for Raoul and Michelle as they figured out some of the more complex sentences. Perhaps another stepped-up small-group lesson for these two could be around building their awareness of time clues, which would help increase their understanding of how multiple characters can be doing multiple things in sentences. Likewise, bringing their awareness to how commas work in these sentences, perhaps through some writing, might reinforce their comprehension.

No matter what texts you use and no matter how many steps you take with students, the bottom line about instructing in stepped-up small groups is to have students focus on problem solving. This is nitty-gritty work about very concrete textual clues, but I am not there to frontload specific textual clues I want students to focus on; turn reading into workbook work; or deliver mini-lectures on pronouns, flashbacks, or cause-and-effect. Stepped-up lessons *by design* allow the know-and-tell teacher inside each of us to step into the wings. We don't have to know and tell because we're setting students up to do so. My role is to simply notice and name as *they* do the work.

Flexible Teaching for Flexible Learning

As always, teaching is an act requiring revision, and stepped-up small groups are a lesson in this. I have often set out, confident and clear, to bring about the instructional path I've worked out and choose the students who would benefit from the small group and the texts I've chosen. But no sooner do I start the group then something happens to remind me that I have to continually keep my eye on the students in front of me. What works in one school might not work in another; what works with some students won't work with others. Students exist to teach this lesson to teachers each and every day. We can't script this work.

I was reminded of this recently when I was working with a group on time clues using the opening of *Tales of a Fourth Grade Nothing*. One of the students referred to the main character as Jimmy. He said that Jimmy had won the turtle and that Jimmy was walking home from the party. Other students in the group politely corrected him, showing the clues they used to infer that the main character's name was Peter. The student saw the clues and agreed with them but continued to call the character Jimmy. I tucked this information into my notes. I knew from my conferences that other students struggled with first-person narrators and with inferring information that was indirectly conveyed. This student would probably benefit more from a small group about one or both of those things rather than continuing to be pulled up my well-planned staircase of increasingly complex time clues. Like a good athlete, I have to be prepared and spontaneous at the same time. If I want my students to be flexible learners, I need to be a flexible learner too.

TOOLBOX ➧ HOW TO PLAN AND IMPLEMENT STEPPED-UP SMALL-GROUP LESSONS

Before:

- Look closely at texts your students are reading.
  - You don't have to read the whole book. Simply read the opening paragraphs or turn to a random middle page.
  - Think about what you know and how you know it, focusing on nitty-gritty textual clues that help with basic comprehension.
  - Make a *What You Know/How You Know It* chart to help you articulate your comprehension (see Appendix 1).
- Look closely at your students.
  - Look at your research conference notes and think about any patterns you notice from your class.
  - Make a chart to solidify your understandings of your students (*Patterns from Conferences/Possible Stepped-Up Lessons*) (see Appendix 5).
  - Plan groups to be no more than four students. Students don't have to be at the same reading level.
- Plan.
  - Look at the *How You Know It* side of the chart you made. These are your possible teaching points.
  - Plan problem-solving questions to emphasize *how* a reader knows what they know, not just *what* they know.
    + "How can we figure out . . . ?"
    + "How can we keep track of . . . ?"
  - Think about logical steps from simple to more complex.
    + Choose no more than three texts for each lesson.
    + Shorter sections of text are more practical than longer ones.
    + The first step for students should be a text with clues that will be relatively easy for those students. This will help them focus on *how* they know what they know, not just *what* they know.
    + The next step should be slightly trickier but not too hard. It can contain some clues that are similar to the ones in the easier text plus some that are more complicated. This will help students move from the familiar to the unfamiliar.
  - Use the suggested planning template (see Appendix 6) to help you focus.
  - Work with colleagues. Look at books together and talk about what you know and how you know it. Share texts with each other.

During:

- Let the students know why you have gathered them together.
- Summarize some of the work you've noticed them doing in their independent reading, emphasizing how they have done that work.
- Frame the lesson around the big work of reading, what this nitty-gritty work will help them do as thinkers.
- Use the problem-solving language you have planned ("how can we . . .", "how do we . . . ?").
- When they answer your questions, don't forget to follow up by asking them how they know what they know.
- Keep your eye on the time.
   ○ A group can be long or short depending on how long the texts are or how many texts you are reading with the students.
      + Two short texts can take about fifteen to twenty minutes.
      + Three short texts might take twenty-five minutes or more.
- Create a chart from student talk (See Appendix 7).
   ○ Label the chart around the problem or question you are asking the students to grapple with.
   ○ As students answer that question by citing specific clues in the text that help them know what they know in a text, try to generalize those clues so they are applicable to other texts. Write those generalizations down as strategies that students can refer to as they step up into harder texts. (See Chapter 6 for more about generalizing textual clues.)
   ○ Use this chart to help you notice and name as you wrap up the group. This is your teaching point and you want to make sure it is clearly stated by the end of your time together.
- Take notes about your students.
   ○ Jot down a few specific words you notice students use during the group. This will help you reflect on next steps after the group is over.
- Consider your "look-for's." Are students exceeding your expectations? Are they not meeting them? Do you have to revise your lesson based on their responses?

After:

- You may want to copy the chart you have created together to give to each student. This will remind them about what to look for as they read independently. If the chart fits on a bookmark, great. If not, it can fit in their reading notebooks or folders.
- Reflect on each student's contribution to the group and think about individual next steps. Jot these down to help you plan follow-up.

- Follow up with students:
    - through check-in conferences;
    - with more steps into more complex texts;
    - through another stepped-up group on a related topic.
- Reflect on the lesson.
    - Did I follow my plan? Why or why not?
    - Did the questions I asked link to my teaching point?
    - Were the texts well chosen for my purpose? Too many? Too few? Too easy? Too hard?
    - Were the students well matched for my purpose—i.e., did they need this?
    - Were my "look for's" accurate? Was I surprised by anything I hadn't anticipated—in the texts or from the students?
    - How was my timing? Too long? Too short?
    - Do I have a doable plan for keeping track of next steps for individual students?
    - Would other students benefit from the same or a similar lesson?
    - Are there any whole-class implications that came up from this group?
    - Can I share some of this work with colleagues and get their input about useful texts and teaching points?

CHAPTER

TEACHING SMARTER
Stepping Students Up to Do More Complex Thinking in Read-Aloud and Shared Reading

A bird doesn't sing because it has an answer. It sings because it has a song.

—Maya Angelou

I stopped into a sixth-grade special education class in Queens where a group of students were huddled around the teacher. The Learning Objective on the board informed me that the class was working to "determine an author's point of view or purpose in a text." You will no doubt recognize this as a Common Core State Standard—it is Standard 6 in

"Reading Informational Texts." Each student had a copy of an article that was many pages long and filled with dense text. As I moved closer I realized it was a text required by the New York City Department of Education as part of an interim assessment designed to prepare students for the state tests.

In addition to the text, each student had a worksheet of questions they were supposed to answer but they were, in fact, doing anything but: One girl kept standing up and wandering around the room; a boy had his hands inside his desk, preoccupied with something; another was trying to get his pencil to work properly. The few others were sitting passively, looking at the teacher. She was being patient, moving from the worksheet to the text, pointing to specific passages for students to focus on, emphasizing words she wanted the students to underline, and coaching them on what to write where.

As I observed the room, a quote by Al Shanker that I had read recently popped into my mind. Decades ago, he described American schools from the point of view of a Martian: they would be, he wrote, places where "five days out of seven adults help children get ready to go to a building where they sit and watch adults work" (Beck and McKeown 2006, 8). The teacher in this room was most definitely working, but what, I wondered, was that work yielding? And the students were indeed sitting and watching the adult work, but what were they supposed to be learning? Specifically what were they learning about author's perspective and, more important, about how to read and why?

I was able to share my concerns with the teacher after class, and she agreed with me. "I know I'm doing all the work," she moaned, "But my students can't understand this text. They can barely decode it. This is a required unit and a required text. What choice do I have?"

Her question was rhetorical, but I went home dissatisfied. Here was a classic example of how standards and standardized assessments have forced teachers to take their eyes off their students, as I described in Chapter 4. And here was a classic example of a teacher's response to those requirements, to act like a mama-bird and do the work *for* her students.

So what choice *do* we have?

Stepped-Up Whole-Class Lessons

Since the students in this sixth-grade class were expected to do big thinking work in a difficult text, and since my goal was to allow the students to do this work without relying on the teacher's meaning, I thought a stepped-up whole-class lesson might be in order.

Just as stepped-up small-group lessons emphasize how a reader knows what he or she knows, a stepped-up whole-class lesson does as well. But instead of emphasizing the specific ways print cues work, as I describe in Chapter 5, whole-class lessons emphasize some of the big thinking readers do as they read—thinking that every student can benefit from, not just a select few.

Thinking about themes and main ideas and considering an author's perspective are examples of such thinking. This is important work in reading, and the Anchor Standards in the CCSS contain such language. Students are frequently asked to "identify" a theme or main idea or "determine" an author's point of view.

But determining and identifying are the tip of the iceberg. They are, in effect, the last thing a reader does after following a much more complex process. First, they must dwell within the text, noticing, holding on to, and connecting details and patterns that help them begin to build an understanding of how the author is showing ideas, feelings, or concepts (Barnhouse and Vinton 2012). Identifying a main idea without first noticing and connecting details is a little like focusing on the score of a basketball game without considering how each pass, each dribble, each play contributes to that score. And although many of us keep track of our favorite team's scores without watching every game, we know that the final score is inextricably linked to how the game was played. What gives us pleasure, moves or excites us, disappoints or enrages us, is watching the game unfold, participating, if you will, in that process.

Much of the reading instruction I observe pays little attention to the process, honing in on only the "final score," the answers that have somehow come to demonstrate achievement. *How* readers know what a main idea or a theme is or *how* they can tell what an author's perspective is remains largely invisible. Additionally, the engagement in the process of reading that is both necessary and satisfying to readers remains largely out of reach for many reluctant readers.

We can't get students to do tip-of-the-iceberg work simply by telling them to do so. Rather, we have to dwell below the surface with them, helping them see how readers do this very invisible, abstract thinking—and how rewarding the process can be. Stepped-up whole-class lessons are one way to do this.

Planning from How We Know What We Know

In planning a stepped-up lesson for this sixth-grade class, I first read the article the students were required to read. The piece was called "Can

Animals Think?" by Eugene Linden and was first published in *Time* maga-
zine (not *Time for Kids*, it should be noted). It was about nine pages long,
with no illustrations and very few headings to break up the dense text. Here
is the opening paragraph:

> *The first time Fu Manchu broke out, zookeepers chalked it up to human
> error. On a balmy day, the orangutans at the Omaha Zoo had been play-
> ing in their big outdoor enclosure. Not long thereafter, shocked keepers
> looked up and saw Fu and his family hanging out in some trees near the
> elephant barn. Later investigation revealed that the door that connects
> the furnace room to the orangutan enclosure was open. Head keeper
> Jerry Stones chewed out his staff, and the incident was forgotten. But the
> next time the weather was nice, Fu Manchu escaped again. Fuming,
> Stones recalls, "I was getting ready to fire someone."* (Linden 1999)

As I read I noticed much that was complex about the text; first and fore-
most, the use of idioms (*broke out, chalked it up to, chewed out*) and some of
the vocabulary (*balmy, investigation, enclosure, incident*), which I knew
would be a challenge for these special ed students, but also for many English
language learners in this and other sixth-grade classes at the school—all of
whom were being required to do this assignment. I also saw the complex
syntax of most of the sentences, many of which begin with subordinate
clauses (*The first time Fu Manchu broke out; On a balmy day; Not long there-
after*) and the last, which contains a participial phrase (*Fuming, Stones
recalls, "I was ready to fire someone."*). These constructions, as we saw from
the small-group work described in Chapter 5, often make it difficult for students to keep track of some of the most basic information being provided in
a text, such as who is doing what.

Filtering what I noticed through a broader lens, that of explicit and implicit
textual clues (see Chapter 2), it was clear to me from the first three sentences
that almost everything I knew, every piece of information I got from the text,
was implied. Simply knowing that Fu Manchu was an orangutan required me
to piece together information from multiple sentences: the mention of his name
in the first sentence, which I had to connect with the *orangutans* mentioned in
the second sentence, which I had to connect to *Fu and his family* in the third
sentence. Phew! The same process was required for me to know that Fu
Manchu lived in a zoo and that he escaped from his enclosure (Figure 6.1).
There is not one clue that directly provides this information, but many.

On the one hand these multiple clues provide a redundancy, discussed in
Chapter 5, which acts as a kind of support: if I don't know what *broke out*

Figure 6.1 To understand the most basic information from the opening sentences of "Can Animals Think?" a reader has to infer by connecting multiple clues in the whole paragraph.

What I Know (from the text)	How I Know It
Fu Manchu is an orangutan	Inferred from multiple clues: *Fu Manchu* (first sentence) + *the orangutans* (second sentence) + *Fu and his family* (third sentence) + *orangutan enclosure* (fourth sentence)
Fu Manchu lives in a zoo	Inferred from multiple clues: *Fu Manchu* (first sentence) + *broke out* (first sentence) + *zookeepers* (first sentence) + *Omaha Zoo* (second sentence) + *outdoor enclosure* (second sentence) + *Fu Manchu is one of the orangutans* (second sentence)
Fu Manchu escaped	Inferred from multiple clues: *Fu Manchu broke out* (first sentence) + *the orangutans had been playing in their big outdoor enclosure* (second sentence) + *Not long thereafter, shocked keepers looked up and saw Fu and his family hanging out in some trees near the elephant barn.* (third sentence) + *door . . . was open* (fourth sentence) + *Fu Manchu escaped again* (sixth sentence)

means, for example, or think it means that Fu Manchu is a teenager with a bad case of acne, I can figure it out or self-correct by reading on and using those additional clues.

But that redundancy is also what makes this text complex. Each sentence provides "partial information," which requires a reader to make "tentative decisions . . . to be confirmed, rejected, or refined as reading progresses" (Goodman 1976, 2). If the first few sentences were written in a more explicit, or stated, style it might provide more complete information right away; it might sound something like this:

Fu Manchu is an orangutan at the Omaha Zoo. One day the zookeeper, Jerry Stones, noticed that Fu and his family were not in their pen. They had escaped. He blamed his staff for leaving the door open.

I wondered, briefly, if I should teach this class how to "get" who's in a piece and what's going on when the clues are implicit rather than explicit. I decided against that, however, knowing that such a lesson would be more appropriate for a small group, since what is explicit for one person is implicit for another. For the whole class, I felt it was more important to address the task they were being asked to do, to "determine the author's point of view."

I read on, trying to do just that. What, I wondered, was Eugene Linden's perspective on whether animals can think—and how would I know it? Initially I looked for explicit clues that might convey the author's perspective, phrases such as *I think* or clear opinion words such as *good* or *incredible*. Why did it surprise me that there were none in this piece? Instead, there were several long anecdotes about animals behaving in clever ways, lots of descriptions of different scientists observing animals, repeated references to how scientific study of animal intelligence has evolved over the past few decades, and, nine long pages later, this head-scratching last paragraph:

What is intelligence anyway? If life is about a perpetuation of a species, and intelligence is meant to serve that perpetuation, then we can't hold a candle to pea-brained sea turtles who predated us and survived the asteroid impact that killed off the dinosaurs. As human history has shown, once minds break free of religious, cultural and physical controls, they burn hot and fast, consuming and altering everything around them. Perhaps this is why higher mental abilities, though present in other creatures, are more circumscribed. Still, it is comforting to realize that other species besides our own can stand back and appraise the world around them, even if their horizons are more constrained than the heady, perilous perspective that is our blessing and curse. (Linden 1999)

High expectations are all well and good. But this, as the desperate special education teacher had noted, was a setup for failure. The standards and curriculum had completely passed over these students.

Nonetheless, there was the task. The teacher and I could rail against the system all we wanted but the students still had to do what they had to do: "determine" the author's perspective and write an essay about how it was conveyed throughout the piece.

As is my habit, I sat down to summarize for myself what I knew about the author's perspective and how I knew it. It is telling that I was (and remain) a little unsure that I got the perspective "right." In fact, I believe if I had been a reader in a classroom that emphasized answers over process and expected me to get an "it" on the first go-around, I would not have been able to do this work successfully.

This is because at this level of text complexity, "determining" an author's perspective is really an act of interpretation, which is a process of drafting and revising, of false starts and dead ends (Barnhouse and Vinton 2012). To come up with an interpretive statement about "Can Animals Think?" I had to read and reread the text, check and cross-check, try out and reject some first drafts and keep working until my statement seemed to fit with all the parts of the text.

Additionally, I can make a good case for my statement, but I'm sure that another reader could make an equally good case for a different statement articulating a different perspective. When working with students on big ideas in complex texts, therefore, it is necessary to reflect the fluidity of what it is to "know," to acknowledge that "knowing" in a text such as this is more accurately "interpreting" or "hypothesizing." In order to help me convey this concept, I therefore revised the headings of the *What I Know/How I Know It* chart I introduced in Chapter 2 (Figure 6.2 and Appendix 8).

The *How I Know It* column on my chart was, in effect, my teaching point. I wanted students to understand that authors convey opinions or perspective through the use of carefully chosen anecdotes and facts and through the use of questioning or challenging others' thinking.

But I knew I couldn't just stand up and deliver a mini-lesson on this. Even if I did manage to make myself clear, I feared that these students would still stare blankly at the complex text in front of them. Instead, I knew that I

Figure 6.2 What I think I know, or interpret, to be the author's perspective from "Can Animals Think?" and how I know it

What I *Think* I Know (Interpret) About Author's Perspective	How I Know It
I think the author thinks that animals can definitely think—and that humans have been slow to figure that out.	The use of anecdotes The use of facts The use of questions at the end

had to set them up to see these textual clues and how they operate in simpler texts. In other words, in order to step them up to this complex text, I was first going to have to step them down—way down.

Problem Solving in Stepped-Down Texts

Just as I do when planning stepped-up small-group lessons, I frame whole-class lessons around a question or problem I want the students to grapple with. This introduces a tone of inquiry and problem solving into the classroom. I don't want to give answers as the teacher; I want to seek answers side by side with the students.

The question I decided on for this class was taken from what the students had been asked to do from the standards. I simply took the standard— "determine an author's point of view or purpose in a text and explain how it is conveyed in the text"—and turned it into a question: "How can readers figure out a writer's point of view on a topic?" I then planned on having students explore this question in a variety of texts, starting with ones in which clues are explicit and ending with the complex, required text.

I started by writing the inquiry question on the board—"How can we figure out an author's point of view in a nonfiction text?"—and created a blank What/How chart (Figure 6.3).

I then wrote out the following sentence on the board:

I love pizza.

Figure 6.3 A chart to help scaffold students to become aware of textual clues that provide information

What We Know (Author's Perspective)	How We Know It

"What do you think the author of this sentence feels about pizza?" I asked the students.

I got a unanimous response that the author loved pizza.

"How do you know?" I asked.

They all agreed that the author states it in the word *love*.

I wrote down their thinking on the chart, using the left-hand or *What We Know* side of the chart to stay specific to the text and using the right-hand or *How We Know It* side to generalize (Figure 6.4). This way of charting allows students to see textual clues and eventually transfer their thinking to stepped-up texts.

Figure 6.4 The beginnings of the chart from a sixth-grade class. The wording in the *How We Know It* column is generalized to apply to all texts, not just the one students are reading at the moment.

What We Know (Author's Perspective)	**How We Know It**
The author loves pizza	Clear opinion words (*love*)

Then I wrote out another sentence:

Every day should be pizza day.

I asked the students the same questions—what the author thinks about pizza and how they know. The students said that the author liked pizza and again said it was stated mostly from the word *should*. I generalized that thinking, adding it to the chart (Figure 6.5).

Figure 6.5 Looking at more complex textual clues. The bold print indicates thinking the students are adding as they read additional texts.

What We Know (Author's Perspective)	**How We Know It**
The author loves pizza	Clear opinion words (*love*)
	Words that suggest a solution (*should*)

I then showed them the following paragraph (which I made up for this purpose, so don't go around quoting these statistics):

Pizza is only served in the cafeteria on Fridays. On Fridays, 90 percent of the students finish their lunch but on other days, only 12 percent of students finish their lunch. Some people think that pizza isn't very nutritious, but kids would eat better and therefore get better nutrition if pizza were served more often.

"OK," I said. "Here's a challenge. Do you see any opinion words like *love* here?"

"No."

"And do you see any words like *should*?"

"No."

"So do we know what this author thinks about pizza?"

The students said the author thought that pizza was "good" and "good for students to eat."

"How do you know?"

They pointed to various textual clues that led them to understand the author's views on pizza: the statistics jumped out at them as did the word *better*, which they recognized as an opinion word. They also pointed to the phrases *Some people think* and *but kids would eat better and therefore get better nutrition if pizza were served more often.* As they pointed to each specific phrase, I tried to generalize or categorize what they were saying so it could apply to all texts (Figure 6.6). I also added on to the example opinion words as they cited different ones.

This took about five minutes. Now it was time to apply these strategies to a real text. I passed out copies of the opening page of *Clean Air* by Andrew Bridges.

Air. It's easy to forget it's there. You can't see it. You can't touch it or smell it. But every few seconds, you breathe it in to stay alive—your body needs the oxygen. And air does more. It moves water around the planet and rains it down to nourish all living things—plants, microbes, and animals. It helps keep Earth warm, and it protects us from the Sun's harmful ultraviolet rays.

But people have been pouring pollutants and greenhouse gases into the air. It's easy to think these pollutants just vanish—yes, into thin air! But add enough of them together and we can all see, smell and feel their effects. We'd better take better care of this precious resource—our air.
(Bridges 2008, 4)

Figure 6.6 Stepping up in complexity and pointing out more complex textual clues (in boldface type)

What We Know (Author's Perspective)	How We Know It
The author loves pizza The author thinks pizza is good and good for students to eat	Clear opinion words (*love,* **better, more**) Words that suggest a solution (*should*) **Facts or statistics that are placed together** **Author states what others think and then disagrees (*but*)** **Little words carry big meaning (*but, only, if*)** **Author describes a result of an action (*therefore, if*)**

I read the piece out loud as students followed along. When I finished reading, some students called out that the author thought it was wrong to pollute air. In order to emphasize the use of textual clues, however, and make those clues visible to all students, I tried to slow their thinking down. I pointed back at the chart and the strategies we had compiled in the *How We Know* column.

"Do you see any opinion words in these paragraphs?" I asked.

They all agreed that the word *better* in the last sentence was an opinion word.

"How about words that suggest a solution?" I prodded.

Students took a little more time to find this one but soon a student volunteered: "I think the last sentence [*We'd better take better care of this precious resource—our air*] but I'm not sure what *we'd* means."

I explained that *we'd* was short for *we had*, at which point everyone agreed that this was, indeed, a statement suggesting a solution.

The teacher and I then organized students into table groups and asked them to look through the other strategies listed on the chart, underlining applicable clues in the text that helped them understand what the author thought. Students then shared with the whole group what clues they had found and how those clues had helped them understand the author's perspective.

Figure 6.7 Moving the students' thinking into a real text with even more complex clues

What We Know (Author's Perspective)	How We Know It
The author loves pizza	Clear opinion words (*love, better, more*)
The author thinks pizza is good and good for students to eat	Words that suggest a solution (*should*)
	Facts or statistics that are placed together
The author thinks air pollution is really bad	Author states what others think and then disagrees (*but*)
The author thinks people need to take care of the air	Little words carry big meaning (*but, only, if*)
	Author describes a result of an action (*therefore, if*)
	Opinions that are placed together

The students did not always have an easy time explaining their thinking, but they were adept at pointing to specific sentences that helped them comprehend. Many of them noticed all the "little words" this author used, especially the word *but*. And about the sentence *It's easy to think these pollutants just vanish—yes, into thin air!*, the students were able to recognize that this was an example of the author stating "what others think" even though it didn't begin with more simply stated words such as, *Some people think.*

I added their thinking to the chart in boldface (Figure 6.7) and as the bell rang indicating the end of the period, one student raised his hand for a last urgent comment, "Look! All the facts are in the first paragraph and all the opinions are in the second paragraph!" I turned back to the text, recognizing that he was right. I shouldn't have been surprised. Whenever we allow students to think, they inevitably notice things we haven't noticed in texts. The teacher added it to the chart as I dashed off to my next class.

Stepping Up in Complexity

The teacher and I met later to discuss the next steps up the ladder of text complexity. There was still a long way to go from the persuasive language of

Clean Air to the subtle use of anecdotes and questions prevalent in "Can Animals Think?" My goal was to teach several more texts in a similar manner, choosing ones that had increasingly subtle or less explicit clues, and adding to the chart. The teacher and I browsed through her classroom library to look for suitable materials. It didn't take long for us to come up with the following:

- A social studies trade book about the Japanese internment camps that conveyed strong opinions about the injustice of the camps. One page we thought we could use employed many of the same techniques we had noticed in the easier texts but additionally used a lot of verbs— *forced, suffered, denied,* and *lost*—that functioned, we realized, as "opinion words" (Figure 6.8).
- A science book that contained a page consisting of nothing but a list of facts (Figure 6.9). As we read over the list, we recognized there was a strong point of view coming across. We realized in order to determine this point of view, we were thinking how these facts went together. Initially, we thought it was about the effects of pollution on the earth, but as we read on, we came to other facts that didn't seem to fit that theory. We had to revise and refine our thinking. This was a process of thinking we thought was important to show students. We also thought the deluge of facts in this piece was similar to how the author of "Can Animals Think?" conveyed his point of view, and so recognized that this would be an important step toward helping them do the thinking in the required text.

Figure 6.8 An excerpt from *How Did This Happen Here?*

President Roosevelt signed Executive Order 9066 on February 19, 1942. An executive order is a rule made by a president. It is like a law that people had to follow. The order gave the government unusual power. They said this power was needed to make the United States safe.

The order was about Japanese Americans who lived in the United States. It said they had to move. They were forced to live in internment camps. These were special camps. The camps kept Japanese Americans closed in. They kept them guarded. The government said that Japanese Americans might be spies for Japan. Henry L. Stimson, the U.S. secretary of war, explained: "We cannot understand or trust . . . [the] Japanese."

People's fears led them to deny Japanese Americans their rights. They lost their freedom. As a result, Japanese Americans suffered a great injustice. (Donlan 2007, 7)

Figure 6.9 Excerpt from *The Great Outdoors: Saving Habitats*

- There are now more than 500 million cars polluting the planet. Traffic fumes contain some of the most harmful substances known.
- In Britain, cleaning up pesticides in water costs £200 ($372) million each year.
- In Australia, 41 mammal species have become extinct over the past 200 years. This is more than anywhere else on Earth. Another 117 are endangered and need to be protected.
- In the past twenty years, nearly 700,000 acres (3,000 square kilometers) of wild habitat have been destroyed in California alone.
- Each year more than two million square miles (five million square kilometers) of forest are cut down around the world. That is an area over half the size of Australia!
- The area that is now called the Nouabale-Ndoki National Park in central Africa is such a remote, wild place that it has no trace of people ever having lived there.
- People live on, farm, fish or mine over 80 percent of all the land on Earth.
- Antarctica is a huge continent—it measures 8.7 million square miles (14 million square kilometers) but has no permanent human population. (Spilsbury 2005, 28)

Figure 6.10 shows the thinking the students did in the social studies text; namely, all the strategies they had previously practiced in the stepped-down texts, plus a new strategy, which was to pay attention to opinion words that might be tricky or disguised, such as verbs.

We expected the science text was most likely going to provide the biggest challenge for these students. This is because they had been taught to identify facts as distinct from opinions, mostly through years of worksheets with titles such as Fact vs. Opinion. Here was a text, like many, where facts are not used in opposition to opinions but in support of opinions. Despite the difficulty of the task we anticipated, I was determined to maintain the methodology of inquiry I had started, allowing students to figure out the problem at hand—namely, how they could figure out the writer's perspective.

I read the "text" (see Figure 6.9) out loud. It didn't take long for them to recognize that this was a different kind of text; indeed it didn't sound like a text at all, but a list. I then reread the What/How charts the students had created from the easier texts, asking them which of these strategies they could apply to this text. They realized that there were no opinion words (though one student noticed the verb *destroyed* and thought that might be an example of a disguised opinion word), no *shoulds* or *buts*, and only one word suggesting a solution (*need*). When I read the strategy about putting facts together, however, they agreed that this was probably the best approach. This was what the teacher and I had hoped, since this was what the students needed to do in "Can Animals Think?"

Figure 6.10 Looking at more complex or "tricky" texts and adding to the chart

What We Know (Author's Perspective)	How We Know It
The author loves pizza The author thinks pizza is good and good for students to eat	Clear opinion words (*love, better, more*) Words that suggest a solution (*should*) Facts that are placed together
The author thinks air pollution is really bad The author thinks people need to take care of the air	Author states what others think and then disagrees (*but*) Little words carry big meaning (*but, only, if*) Author describes a result of an action (*therefore, if*) Opinions that are placed together
The author thinks the Japanese should not have been put in internment camps	**Words that convey opinions are sometimes tricky. Look at verbs (actions), not just adjectives (descriptions)**

The teacher and I asked students to work in groups to come up with a statement about how they thought these facts fit together and then circulated among the students as they worked. Several students responded almost immediately, as if this were a race to a finish line. They stated confidently that the author thought "pollution was bad." This was exactly what the teacher and I had thought when we had first read the list. Another student said that the author was "excited." When I asked him what information in the text led him to think that, he pointed to the exclamation point in the fifth bullet, *That is an area over half the size of Australia!*

I realized for the thousandth time that when inexperienced readers are asked to do big-thinking work in texts, such as determining an author's perspective or finding a main idea or theme, they often pick out one piece of information that is the most available to them—in this case, a punctuation mark, but in many other cases, a detail or a section from a text—rather than think about the entire text.

"Remember," I interrupted the students, "Your job isn't to tell us what the author thinks—at least not yet. Your job right now is to think about how *all* the facts might fit together. So, talk with your groups and see if each fact fits with your idea."

Students treated this activity as a kind of puzzle. "How does this fit?" they asked each other, "How does that fit?" As they worked they negotiated answers, returning again and again to the text to reconsider. This was exactly what we wanted. Students were *figuring out* the author's perspective by paying close attention to the text, they were not *identifying* it. And they were seeing firsthand that synthesizing—putting parts together—is not a clean, linear process that some readers are able to do while others aren't; rather, it's a messy, complicated process that requires many drafts and much revision.

This was the bottom of the iceberg work that these students desperately needed. They had had years of mama-bird teaching, teaching that was about the answers rather than the process by which those answers were constructed. They had therefore come to believe that texts have right or wrong answers and, tragically, that those answers were not within their reach. But here they recognized that answers are built through an active process of putting parts together—and that process can be kind of fun.

We added these important understandings to the chart in boldface type (Figure 6.11) in an attempt to make their revisions visible. We also chose this time to revise the heading of the chart to highlight the process of moving through uncertainty toward interpretation.

The Final Step Up

After this lesson, the teacher and I thought we could take students back to the required text—the final step up in this series of stepped-up lessons. Stamina in the nine-page "Can Animals Think?" was still going to be a challenge, but with some careful chunking, the teacher continued on her journey through this text with the students. This time, instead of pointing to *her* understanding as they read, she pointed to the strategies they had seen in the easier texts, strategies that were now hanging visibly on a chart in the room.

When they came upon this paragraph, for example, they didn't know all of the words (*elusive* and *formation*), but looking over the chart, they recognized that the paragraph was most likely an example of how the "author states what others think and disagrees." The use of the word *some* in the phrase *The very question offends some philosophers and scientists* was their clue.

Figure 6.11 Adding on to name the processes of thinking involved in interpreting complex texts

Think **What We ^ We Know (*Interpret*)** **(Author's Perspective)**	**How We Know It**
The author loves pizza The author thinks pizza is good and good for students to eat	Clear opinion words (*love, better, more*) Words that suggest a solution (*should*) Facts that are placed together
The author thinks air pollution is really bad The author thinks people need to take care of the air	Author states what others think and then disagrees (*but*) Little words carry big meaning (*but, only, if*) Author describes a result of an action (*therefore, if*) Opinions that are placed together
The author thinks the Japanese should not have been put in internment camps	Words that convey opinions are sometimes tricky. Look at verbs (actions), not just adjectives (descriptions)
The author thinks that ~~pollution is bad~~ humans have messed up the earth	**We think about how facts fit together** **We draft and revise our ideas as we keep reading, to look at all parts of a text, not just some parts of it**

Over the years I have written several articles and two books on animal-intelligence experiments and the controversy that surrounds them. I have witnessed at close range the problems scientists encounter when they try to examine phenomena as elusive as language and idea formation. Do animals really have thoughts, what we call consciousness? The very question offends some philosophers and scientists, since it cuts so close to what separates men from beasts. (Linden 1999)

As for that tricky last paragraph, which follows, students still had no idea what the author was talking about (I have to confess, I'm with them). They did, however, float the possibility that this was like the last paragraph in the text *Clean Air*, where the author "saved all his opinions for the last paragraph."

> *What is intelligence anyway? If life is about a perpetuation of a species, and intelligence is meant to serve that perpetuation, then we can't hold a candle to pea-brained sea turtles who predated us and survived the asteroid impact that killed off the dinosaurs. As human history has shown, once minds break free of religious, cultural and physical controls, they burn hot and fast, consuming and altering everything around them. Perhaps this is why higher mental abilities, though present in other creatures, are more circumscribed. Still, it is comforting to realize that other species besides our own can stand back and appraise the world around them, even if their horizons are more constrained than the heady, perilous perspective that is our blessing and curse. (Linden 1999)*

So, what are those opinions? What did the students eventually "determine" the author's perspective to be in "Can Animals Think?" They came to a general consensus that the author thinks that animals *can* think. And when it came time for them to write the required essay about how the author *develops* his argument, they had only to turn to the charts we had created together for support, charts that had come entirely from thinking *they* had done.

Summary

Stepped-up whole-class lessons can be done in any grade and around any of the big thinking that readers do and that tends to be invisible. Just as I did with this lesson, teachers can introduce lessons in any grade using problem-solving language. With younger students who may be encountering texts requiring inferring, I often ask, "How can we figure out something if it's not stated in a text?" (see the language I used in Chapter 3 with Daniel, the second grader reading *Frog and Toad*). With older students, I often phrase inquiry questions around an author's craft or technique ("Why all this imagery?" or "How can we make sense of the structure of this piece?").

I also employ problem-solving language while preparing kids for standardized tests, since many questions ask students to identify themes, main ideas, or the author's message or purpose—and since many students struggle mightily with these questions, especially in test-level texts. I first work with students in stepped-down texts, charting how they know what they know, and then continue to refer to and build on that work as I step them into subsequent, more complex, test-level texts.

Stepped-up lessons, whether they are designed to teach nitty-gritty textual clues as described in Chapter 5 or clues that help readers construct big-idea thinking, are useful ways to teach by *revealing* rather than *telling*. My propensity to mama-bird can therefore be put to rest—for my benefit as well as that of my students.

TOOLBOX ⟶ HOW TO DO WHOLE-CLASS STEPPED-UP LESSONS AROUND BIG-THINKING WORK IN BOOKS

Planning:

- Start at the top step.
  - ○ Start with a text that you know is complex or required for your students. This can include some texts that are at the levels you know will be on the test or some of the text exemplars that appear by grade in Appendix B of the Common Core materials.
  - ○ Ask yourself what you know, particularly around big-thinking work, such as author's perspective, theme, or main idea.
  - ○ Ask yourself how you know what you know, paying close attention to the textual clues that the author is using to convey those ideas.
  - ○ Organize your thinking by making a *What I Know (or Interpret)/How I Know It* chart (Appendices 1 and 8).
- Step down—way down.
  - ○ Look at what you wrote in the *What I Know* column of your chart. Think about the most obvious or explicit ways that an author could convey those ideas.
  - ○ Find (or write) a text (or sentence) that uses these obvious clues. Remember, this work is not about the Lexile or Fountas and Pinnell level of the text; it's about specific textual clues that you want to highlight for students' thinking.
- Find middle-step texts.
  - ○ Open lots of books. Read the first few paragraphs or pages. Turn to a random page in the middle.
  - ○ Think about what you know and how you know it.
  - ○ Construct *What I Know/How I Know It* charts to help you clarify your thinking. Try to generalize the language in the *How I Know It* column

so it's applicable to multiple texts (see examples in Figures 6.4, 6.5, 6.6, 6.7, 6.10, and 6.11). These will become your teaching points.

○ Work with colleagues. Collaborating on finding appropriate texts for your students is productive and enlightening work to do in grade teams. This is especially interesting to do in teams when drafting a unit to help your students prepare for standardized tests.

○ Depending on your students, you will want to choose three or four texts on a continuum from the most obvious to the most complex.

Keeping in mind that complexity is a relative concept—in the eye of the beholder, as it were—some general "look-for's" to help guide your choices appear in Figure 6.12.

Teaching:

• Introduce the lesson as a problem to be solved. Instead of a learning objective worded like a statement, turn it into a question. Examples:

○ Instead of: "Students will be able to identify a theme"
Ask: "How can we figure out themes?"

○ Instead of: "Students will determine author's perspective"
Ask: "How can we figure out author's perspective if it's not stated?"

• Create a two-column chart: *What We Know/How We Know It.*

○ The *What We Know* column is for charting specific ideas from the texts that the students know. (Example: *We know the author loves pizza.*)

○ The *How We Know It* column is for you to try to generalize the textual clues students are using. (Example: A student points to the word *love* in the text and you write *opinion words* on the chart.)

• Each time you introduce a new text to the students, review the strategies in the *How We Know It* column so students will be more aware of looking for those clues as they read. Add on to the chart, as needed, with new clues and/or new examples.

• Recognize with the students that the clues may be getting more and more complex, requiring them to add on or expand their understanding of previous examples. (Example: *verbs can be opinion words.*)

• Recognize, too, that what they "know" from the more complex texts may not be as immediately recognizable, or they may begin to disagree or have different interpretations. When this happens, notice it with the students and revise your chart to read *What We Think We Know* or *What We Interpret.*

○ Make the process of interpretation visible for the students in complex texts by focusing on one strategy at a time. (Example: "Let's work on

Figure 6.12 Some general "look-for's" about how ideas are conveyed to help guide stepped-up text choices

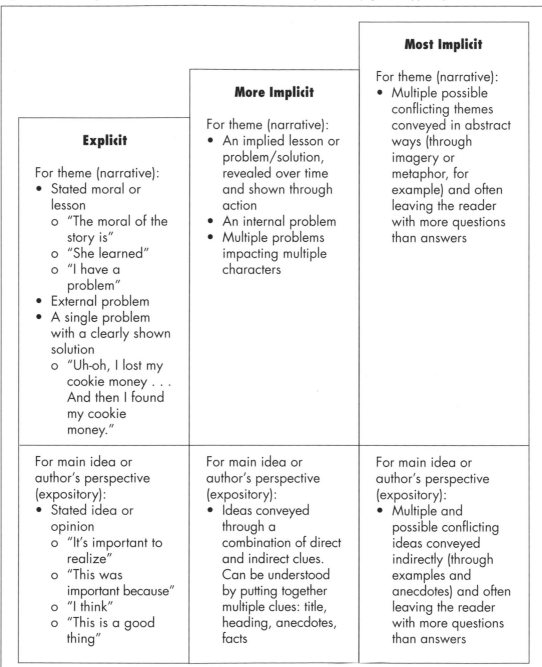

Explicit

For theme (narrative):
- Stated moral or lesson
  - "The moral of the story is"
  - "She learned"
  - "I have a problem"
- External problem
- A single problem with a clearly shown solution
  - "Uh-oh, I lost my cookie money . . . And then I found my cookie money."

More Implicit

For theme (narrative):
- An implied lesson or problem/solution, revealed over time and shown through action
- An internal problem
- Multiple problems impacting multiple characters

Most Implicit

For theme (narrative):
- Multiple possible conflicting themes conveyed in abstract ways (through imagery or metaphor, for example) and often leaving the reader with more questions than answers

For main idea or author's perspective (expository):
- Stated idea or opinion
  - "It's important to realize"
  - "This was important because"
  - "I think"
  - "This is a good thing"

For main idea or author's perspective (expository):
- Ideas conveyed through a combination of direct and indirect clues. Can be understood by putting together multiple clues: title, heading, anecdotes, facts

For main idea or author's perspective (expository):
- Multiple and possible conflicting ideas conveyed indirectly (through examples and anecdotes) and often leaving the reader with more questions than answers

fitting these facts together before we think about what the author's perspective may be.")

○ Don't forget to also notice, name, and chart the process of thinking you see students doing as they work (Example: "drafting and revising" or "puzzling" or saying, "maybe"). This process can be added to the *How We Know It* column of the chart.

Teacher's Role in Stepped-Up Work:

• Read the required texts. Consider what you know and how you know it.
• Choose or write texts that step students *down* from the most complex text.
• Use problem-solving language when introducing the lesson.
• Elicit from students not just *what* they know but *how* they know it.
• Generalize and chart student thinking as they explain.
  ○ Remember: The charts are coconstructed side by side with the students, not preconstructed.
• Celebrate students' accomplishments and engagement.

Student's Role in Stepped-Up Work:

• Read
• Think
• Talk
• Think some more
• Share meaning, insight, and clues
• Read some more
• Apply *how you know* strategies to other texts
• Bask in the satisfaction of intellectual work well done.

Reminder: Don't mama-bird. Don't tell students what to think or point to clues *you* get but *they* may not. If they are not getting complex clues, back up and think about stepping down again to help make those clues and the role they play in texts more visible the next time.

CONCLUSION
On Standards, Standardization, and Agency

All serious daring starts from within.

—Eudora Welty

The great American short story writer Eudora Welty has written a marvelous autobiography called *One Writer's Beginnings*. I was first drawn to this book as a graduate student studying writing because it is more than the story of Welty's life; it is a guide about the process of writing, organized around three chapters, "Listening," "Learning to See," and "Finding a Voice." After describing in the first two chapters how she learned to listen and see, Welty talks about how those actions helped her find her voice as a writer:

> *Connections slowly emerge. . . . Experiences too indefinite of outline in themselves to be recognized for themselves connect and are identified as a larger shape. And suddenly a light is thrown back, as when your train*

makes a curve, showing that there has been a mountain of meaning ris-
ing behind you on the way you've come, is rising there still, proven now
through retrospect. (Welty 1983, 90)

In reading and rereading Welty's book, it becomes clear that the process
she describes is not just applicable to writing but also to reading. We burrow
into a book, its details not immediately recognizable as meaningful, but as
we keep reading—listening, seeing—what we have already read begins to
fall into place, coming into a kind of clarity. "We read forward and think
back," is how Vicki Vinton and I put it in *What Readers Really Do*
(Barnhouse and Vinton 2012, 113).

This process also seems to describe teaching. As I wrote in Chapter 1,
the most important part of our job is to pay attention. We have to learn to
listen and see before the "mountain of meaning" becomes clear.
Unfortunately, this is a time when listening and seeing have become lost arts
in schools. As standardized, summative assessments bear more weight than
individualized, formative ones, there are few encouragements to pause and
reflect, to hear beyond chatter and see beyond the churn.

But I believe if we do listen, our voices will be more authentic and
insightful. This book was born out of just such a pause. I pulled a chair next
to first one student and then another and simply listened as they read. I did-
n't talk, though the teacher was watching me, and the students themselves
seemed to expect me to fill those moments with what I knew or thought I
knew. I had to give myself permission to pay attention.

Eventually what I noticed gave rise to words—these words—but I would
be a terrible teacher indeed if I saw this book as the end of a closed cycle. If
I have learned anything from that first pause, it is that listening and noticing
are recursive, part of a deepening cycle. The more we see and hear, the better we get at seeing and hearing; our work deepens, becomes more inten-
tional, our voices evolve.

Above all, I hope that this book helps you deepen what you notice. I
hope in doing so that your students will deepen what they notice—in books,
yes, but also in their everyday lives. Maxine Greene calls such noticing a
"wide-awakeness" (Greene 1977, 121), and expresses in no uncertain terms
its importance in education: "Consciousness doesn't come automatically,"
she writes, "it comes through being alive, awake, curious, and often furious"
(Greene 2008).

That's what we need to teach students: to develop consciousness by paying attention. In the broadest sense of the term, this is what reading is: constructing ah-ha! moments out of all that's to be noticed in a text. One cannot

do such thinking without understanding that the process matters—what one notices matters and what one thinks matters. In other words, one cannot do such thinking without agency.

What can be more important for a child to learn in school?

In this age of standards I believe we need to cultivate agency in order to keep our classrooms from becoming standardized. If we think of standards not as norms or specific levels that have to be achieved but as expectations about how to think, we can set a bar in our classrooms where students learn and practice listening and seeing, where they develop "wide-awakeness." From this process they will learn that their thinking matters—they will develop agency—which in turn, will cause them to engage in deeper thinking and result in more complex thoughts.

In contrast, if we emphasize standardization, which requires specific books to be read and specific assessments to be passed, the students' thoughts will be valued over their process of thinking. Are they correct? Do they match? The thoughts will become severed from the thinking, and the essence of thinking—agency—will be lost.

Our job as teachers of reading is not to teach students The Text, which teaches standardization, but to teach students how to enter a text, absorb it, and experience it. To teach this process we have to teach for engagement. We cannot pluck details or elements or lessons or main ideas out of a text and think that our students will have gotten "it." Reading is something active we do, a process. We immerse ourselves in texts. We dive into their words, which make up sentences and pages that call out to us to be turned and then mysteriously unfold into ideas, touching us and impacting our lives. This process matters; the act of reading is part and parcel of the meaning itself.

Furthermore, because this process is a "self-extending" one (Clay 1991), the more we do it the better we get at it. Several well-designed studies have confirmed this concept, dubbed the "Matthew-effect" after a passage in the Bible about the rich getting richer and the poor getting poorer. Most famously, Anne Cunningham and Keith Stanovich (2001) conducted a study that led them to conclude that "the very act of reading can help children compensate for modest levels of cognitive ability . . . that is, reading will make them smarter" (147). On the other end of the spectrum, they found that through a "combination of deficient decoding skills, lack of practice, and difficult materials," less skilled students often had more "unrewarding reading experiences," thereby getting caught in a cycle where "practice is avoided or merely tolerated without real cognitive involvement" (137). Not reading, it appears, is also a self-extending process.

The phrase "without real cognitive involvement" from that study is the heartbreaker for me because it is exactly the opposite of Maxine Greene's "alive, awake, curious and furious." It also provides an implicit challenge to teachers, a kind of catch-22. If readers learn to read by reading, how can we teach nonreaders? How do we break the avoidance cycle? How do we make sure that reading will yield a reward for these students, that whatever effort they put into the words and pages will result in a palpable payoff?

To some extent, the answer is about book choice. We need to give students many opportunities to read books in many different scenarios (Kittle 2013). Can they read books that are above their level? Absolutely. Is that all they should read? Absolutely not. Should they read texts of their choice? A resounding yes. Can they read texts chosen for them? Yes, again. Students—all students—need all of the above and in varying amounts.

What they don't need is a single diet.

We can ensure that this doesn't happen by looking closely at our students' reading opportunities. Are they all determined for them—by a teacher, a publisher, or a program? Are they all "aligned" with the Common Core State Standards or excerpted or anthologized in textbooks? Do they all come loaded with comprehension questions, activities, and preset lessons?

If so, warns Tom Newkirk, reading has been "transformed from an experience to a task. It concludes not with that special feeling of literary closure—but with a set of comprehension assignments. Readers lose the sense of autonomy they experience when reading texts in the original venue, on their own terms" (Newkirk 2008). In other words, the use of such texts results in reading without agency, an oxymoron if ever there was one.

Yet still the use of single-diet, skill-based programs and anthologies prevails. Choice and independence are being whittled away from curricula despite the evidence that independent reading improves skills and cognitive ability (Krashen 2004), that choice and engagement positively impact strategic learning behaviors (Ivey and Johnston 2013), and that as students move into middle and high school they do less reading, not more, at home *and* in school (Scholastic 2013). Pearson's ReadyGen program (Pearson 2014), for example, purchased in 2013 by the New York City Department of Education for use in elementary schools, contains what is called "independent practice" but is really only a time allotted for students to revisit the whole-class text. These texts have been chosen to match the exemplars provided in Appendix B of the CCSS, meaning they are far above the level at which most students can be expected to have "independent and proficient" cognitive involvement. This and other similar programs and curricula seem to have been created with some kind of magical thinking—that by simply raising the level of texts students are exposed to, the standards will somehow be achieved.

I, for one, don't buy it. I don't buy it because I believe that as agency decreases so does engagement and as engagement decreases so does learning. Anyone who has walked into a classroom of disengaged students, whether they are kindergartners or twelfth graders, knows that this is not a viable model for education.

But I've learned from visiting a range of classrooms, grades K-12, from New York to California, that choice and independence can look like many things: it can look like students reading the same book for some amount of time and then having time to read independently in a book of their own choosing; it can look like students having a choice of genre or topic to read within; it can look like students choosing a book to read with a reading partner or choosing from among a variety of options for a book club or choosing what to read for homework or for a drop-everything-and-read period.

More important than a particular structure, choice and independence have as their backbone cognitive involvement. In reading, this means that no matter what books our students are reading, we facilitate opportunities where they can notice and think about what they notice. It's as simple as that.

In an eighth-grade class in Colorado, for example, I happened to be visiting on the day the teacher was introducing a whole-class novel, *The Book Thief* by Markus Zusak (2007). She knew the book was going to pose a challenge for her students and thought that to help them comprehend the opening pages, she would reveal upfront the fact that the book is narrated by Death. I asked her if she wouldn't mind experimenting that day; would it be OK if we read the opening pages to the students and simply asked them what they noticed and what questions they had (Barnhouse and Vinton 2012)? She graciously agreed, and we hunkered down to listen as the students shared in table groups.

Students noticed a lot: the references to color and chocolate, and the fact that the narrator repeatedly used the word *humans* to refer to people. They noticed what they called "violent" words (*punctured hearts, beaten lungs, leftover humans*), and several groups homed in on the line *Your soul will be in my arms*. Moving from groups to the whole class, students voiced questions they still had, and discussion revolved around whether the story was being told by a serial killer or perhaps some kind of graveyard dweller.

This, of course, was exactly what the teacher thought the students needed to "get" from the text, yet they ended up not needing her to provide this information. Rather, they drew conclusions from details they noticed, constructing meaning through choice and independence. They were thus perfectly poised to continue closely reading this complex text. They would surely keep noticing deeply as they read on, refining their understanding and eventually concluding not just that the narrator of this text is Death but perhaps also why the author might have made that choice and what ideas that allowed him to explore.

Transforming your teaching from explaining to listening is a small, deceptively simple step. You can start tomorrow. You don't have to change your curriculum or units of study or the books you are teaching. Like the teacher in Colorado, you simply have to change how you see your students. If you treat them as meaning makers, they will act like meaning makers.

The important thing is that we seize the opportunities we have. As a consultant, I have been forced to learn this. My windows of opportunity are even narrower than those of the classroom teachers with whom I work. It is the nature of my work to move around, to cycle in and out of schools. I may see a student only a handful of times in a school year; I may see a student once. I have no choice but to delve right into listening mode. I had one conversation with Nora, for example. That was it. I never returned to her classroom. Yet listening to her revealed thinking that changed the way I teach.

Sometimes it's not me who moves on but the students. After Hurricane Sandy damaged one of the schools I work in, displacing the students for several months, I returned, hoping to follow up with one particular student. I didn't find him in class that day. "Absent?" I asked the teacher. "No, gone," he replied. "Gone? Where?" I asked. "Who knows? Maybe the Bronx. Maybe Pennsylvania."

While events like Sandy don't happen every day (knock on wood), there are countless other issues that sweep through our students' lives—issues regarding family and custody, employment, housing and homelessness, foster care, and immigration. We have to listen while we can.

And we have to use books as our partners in this work.

Not anthologies, not "text-dependent" comprehension questions, not standards, and certainly not tests.

Books.

We have to use books, of course, because they speak to issues that students face in their lives. They allow readers to navigate thorny choices, to consider new ways of thinking about a problem, to see the consequences of a behavior or discover a new idea.

Books also allow readers to imagine "otherness." In picking up *Cat in the Hat* as a child, for example (Seuss 1957), I most certainly learned how to decode the 220 rhyming words that appear between those covers. But I also learned that those words were an invitation to jump into the story, enabling me to temporarily become each of the characters: I could be the fish who is the worrier and the voice of reason, or the children, mysteriously abandoned by their well-heeled mother, one moment bored, the next torn between gut-wrenching right and wrong. I could even become the cat, living a life of reckless abandon for a few delicious moments.

This, I believe, is what it means to make text-to-self connections: to lose ourselves in an experience in order to find ourselves, transformed.

But we also need books simply because the act of reading teaches us that we can be meaning makers.

"Read it again," a child pleads. "Again. Again."

Why?

She already knows what happens, she knows the ending, she practically knows every word by heart. But she insists on reading it again. I believe this is because the experience of reading—noticing and constructing meaning— helps us understand how to be agents in our lives. To paraphrase Eudora Welty, when readers listen and see, they find their voices.

My older daughter's first full day of kindergarten was on 9/11; her school was three blocks north of the World Trade Center. When a new location was eventually found in another school several miles uptown and it came time to start school again, we were both filled with trepidation: a new subway stop, a new neighborhood, fifty-plus kids, most of whom she didn't know, crowding into one classroom. As we entered that room, she clung to my hand. But through the chaos something caught her eye and I felt her hand relax. "Look, Mom," she said, pointing to a book bin across the room, *"Caps for Sale!"* And just like that she was gone, ready for her second first day of kindergarten.

Books can do that for each of us and for each of our students; they can accompany us as we venture into unknown territories. They do so not only because they tell stories that can guide us but also because the act of reading gives us agency. This, I believe, is the real "so what" and "why bother" of reading, and this, I believe, is what is largely absent from prepared curricula and programs that promise skill improvement and alignment with tests. As teachers, we need to "dare," again pulling from Eudora Welty, to give each of our students the opportunity to develop relationships with books that will allow them to see how to live agentive lives. We can start doing so simply by ensuring that every time our students open a book they know their thinking is valued. They are finding their voices and we are listening.

APPENDIX 1 Template to Help Plan and Implement Instruction Based on What You Notice in Texts

What I Know (from the text)	How I Know It

APPENDIX 2 Template to Help Students Visualize Moving From Confusion to Clarity by Making Within-Text Connections

Huh? (Maybe)	⟷	Oh! (Ah-ha!)

Readers Front & Center: Helping All Students Engage with Complex Texts by Dorothy Barnhouse. Copyright © 2014. Stenhouse Publishers.

APPENDIX 3 A Book/Brain Chart to Help with Instruction That Notices and Names

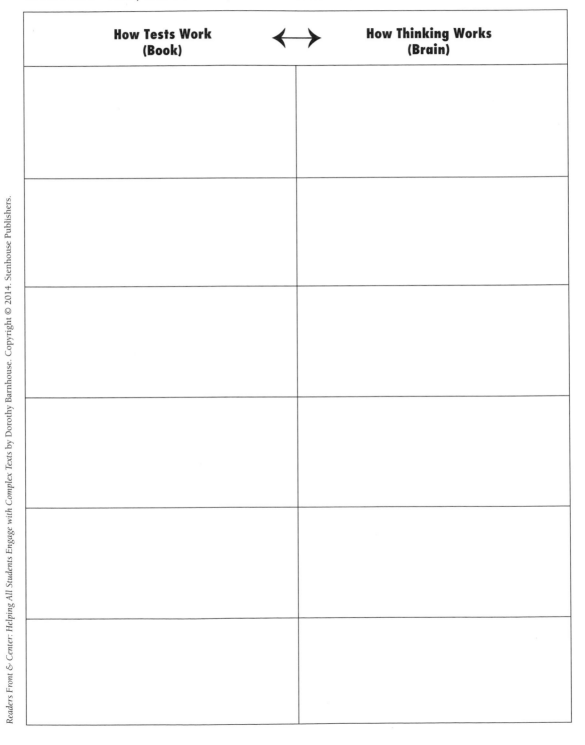

APPENDIX 4 Template for Note Taking During Conferences

Student Name, Date, Book Title, Page No.	What Student Says and Does	Textual Clues Student Uses	Possible Next Steps
_____ _____ _____			
_____ _____ _____			
_____ _____			

Readers Front & Center: Helping All Students Engage with Complex Texts by Dorothy Barnhouse. Copyright © 2014. Stenhouse Publishers.

APPENDIX 5 Template to Help Plan and Implement Instruction Based on Patterns You Notice from Conferences

Patterns from Conferences	Possible Stepped-Up Teaching Points

APPENDIX 6 Template for Planning Stepped-Up Small-Group Reading Instruction

Teaching point for today's group:

How this helps with reading:

Resources (Texts to Use):

Step 1:

Step 2:

Step 3:

What I'll say/ask (How-can-we-figure-out questions):

What I'll look for:

Step 1:

Step 2:

Step 3:

Assessment/Application/Follow-up:

Student Name	What the Student Does/Says	Possible Next Steps

APPENDIX 7 Template for Cocreating Inquiry Charts with Students

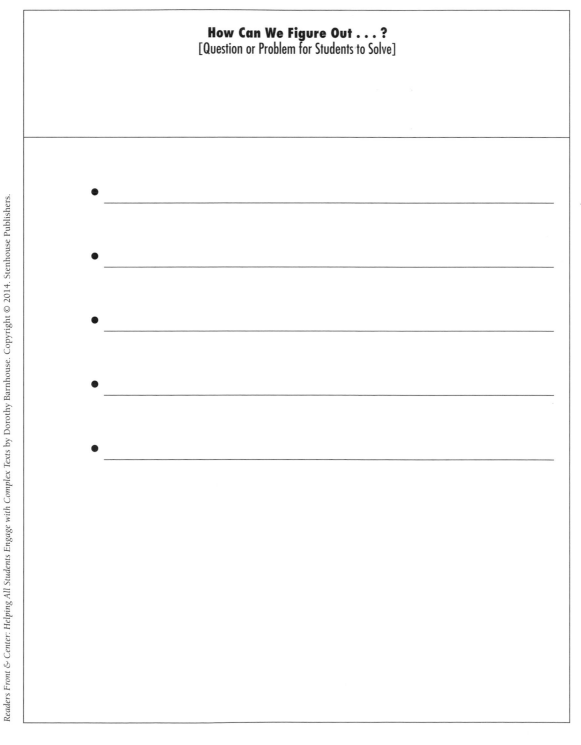

How Can We Figure Out . . . ?
[Question or Problem for Students to Solve]

APPENDIX 8 Template to Make More Complex Thinking Visible in More Complex Texts

What I *Think* I Know (Interpret)	How I Know It

REFERENCES

Adichie, Chimamanda. 2009. "The Danger of a Single Story." Available online at http://www.ted.com/talks/chimamanda_adichie_the_danger_of_a_single_story.html.

Allington, Richard. 2001. *What Really Matters for Struggling Readers: Designing Research-Based Programs*. New York: Longman.

Barnhouse, Dorothy, and Vicki Vinton. 2012. *What Readers Really Do*. Portsmouth, NH: Heinemann.

Beck, Isabel L., and Margaret McKeown. 2006. *Improving Comprehension Using Questioning the Author: A Fresh and Expanded View of a Powerful Theory and Practice*. New York: Scholastic.

Blau, Sheridan. 2003. *The Literature Workshop: Teaching Texts and Their Readers*. Portsmouth, NH: Heinemann.

Blume, Judy. 1972. *Tales of a Fourth Grade Nothing*. New York: Puffin Books.

Bomer, Randy. 2011. *Building Adolescent Literacy in Today's English Classrooms*. Portsmouth, NH: Heinemann.

Bridges, Andrew. 2008. *Clean Air*. New York: Roaring Brook Press.

Bruner, Jerome. 1996. *The Culture of Education*. Cambridge, MA: Harvard University Press.

Calkins, Lucy McCormick. 1994. *The Art of Teaching Writing*. 2nd ed. Portsmouth, NH: Heinemann.

———. 2001. *The Art of Teaching Reading*. New York: Longman.

Cazden, Courtney. 1992. "Revealing and Telling: The Socialization of Attention in Learning to Read and Write." *Educational Psychology* 12: 305–313.

Clay, Marie. 1991. *Becoming Literature: The Construction of Inner Control*. Portsmouth, NH: Heinemann.

———. 2001. *Change Over Time in Children's Literacy Development*. Portsmouth, NH: Heinemann.

Cleary, Beverly. 1975. *Ramona the Brave*. New York: Avon Books.

Coleman, David, and Susan Pimentel. 2012. *Revised Publishers' Criteria for the Common Core State Standards in English Language Arts and Literacy, Grades 3–12.* http://www.corestandards.org/assets/Publishers_Criteria_for_3-12.pdf.

Collins, Kathy. 2004. *Growing Readers: Units of Study in the Primary Classroom.* Portland, ME: Stenhouse.

Common Core State Standards Initiative. 2012a. *Common Core State Standards for English Language Arts & Literacy in History/Social Studies, Science, and Technical Subjects: Appendix A: Research Supporting Key Elements of the Standards.* http://www.corestandards.org/assets/Appendix_A.pdf. http://www.corestandards.org/assets/E0813_Appendix_A_New_Research_on_Text_Complexity.pdf.

Common Core State Standards Initiative. 2012b. *Common Core State Standards for English Language Arts & Literacy in History/Social Studies, Science, and Technical Subjects: Appendix B: Test Examplars and Sample Performance Tasks.* http://www.corestandards.org/assets/Appendix_B.pdf.

Common Core State Standards Initiative. 2012c. "English Language Arts Standards: College and Career Readiness Standards for Reading: 10." http://www.corestandards.org/ELA-Literacy/CCRA/R/10.

Cunningham, Ann, and Keith Stanovich. 2001. "What Reading Does for the Mind." *Journal of Direct Instruction* 1 (2): 137–49.

Curtis, Christopher Paul. 1999. *Bud, Not Buddy.* New York: Random House.

Daniels, Harvey. 2002. *Literature Circles: Voice and Choice in the Student-Centered Classroom.* 2nd ed. Portland, ME: Stenhouse.

Dhami, Narinder. 2003. *Bindi Babes.* New York: Random House.

DiCamillo, Kate. 2000. *Because of Winn-Dixie.* Somerville, MA: Candlewick Press.

———. 2006. *Tiger Rising.* Cambridge, MA: Candlewick Press.

Donlan, Leni. 2007. *How Did This Happen Here?* Chicago: Raintree.

Dr. Seuss. 1957. *The Cat in the Hat.* Boston: Houghton Mifflin.

Dunham, Philip J., Frances Dunham, and Ann Curwin. 1993. "Joint Attentional States and Lexical Acquisition at 18 months." *Developmental Psychology* 29 (5): 827–31.

Dweck, Carol. 2006. *Mindset: The New Psychology of Success.* New York: Random House.

Fisher, Douglas, and Nancy Frey. 2012. *Engaging the Adolescent Learner: Text Dependent Questions.* International Reading Association. http://www.reading.org/Libraries/members-only/FisherFrey_-_Text_Dependent_Questions_-_April_2012.pdf.

Fountas, Irene, and Gay Su Pinnell. 1996. *Guided Reading: Good First Reading for All Children.* Portsmouth, NH: Heinemann.

———. 2012. *The F&P Text Level Gradient: Revision to Recommended Grade-Level Goals.* https://www.heinemann.com/fountasandpinnell/pdfs/WhitePaperTextGrad.pdf.

Gallas, Karen. 1994. *The Languages of Learning: How Children Talk, Write, Dance, Draw, and Sing Their Understanding of the World.* New York: Teachers College Press.

Gawande, Atul. 2013. "Slow Ideas." *The New Yorker,* July 29. http://www.newyorker.com/reporting/2013/07/29/130729fa_fact_gawande.

Goodman, Kenneth S. 1976. *Reading: A Psycholinguistic Guessing Game.* Newark, DE: International Reading Association.

———. 1991. "Whole Language: What Makes It Whole?" In *Literacy in Process: The Heinemann Reader*, ed. Brenda M. Power and Ruth S. Hubbard. Portsmouth, NH: Heinemann.

———. 1996. *Ken Goodman on Reading.* Portsmouth, NH: Heinemann.

Goodman, Yetta. 2008. "Retrospective Miscue Analysis: An Overview." http://www.rcowen.com/WordDocs/RMA-OverviewChapter.doc.

Graves, Donald. 1994. *A Fresh Look at Writing.* Portsmouth, NH: Heinemann.

Greene, Maxine. 1977. "Toward Wide-Awakeness: An Argument for the Humanities in Education." Teachers College Record 79 (1). http://www.maxinegreene.org/pdf/articles/toward_wide_wakeness.pdf.

———. 2008. "The Importance of Personal Reflection." http://www.edutopia.org/maxine-greene-daring-dozen-2008.

Ivey, Gay, and Peter Johnston. 2013. "Engagement with Young Adult Literature: Outcomes and Processes." *Reading Research Quarterly* 48 (3): 255–75.

Johnston, Peter. 2004. *Choice Words.* Portland, ME: Stenhouse.

———. 2012. *Opening Minds.* Portland, ME: Stenhouse.

Kinney, Jeff. 2010. *Diary of a Wimpy Kid: The Ugly Truth.* New York: Abrams.

Kittle, Penny. 2013. *Book Love: Developing Depth, Stamina, and Passion in Adolescent Readers.* Portsmouth, NH: Heinemann.

Klein, Abby. 2004. *Ready Freddy: Tooth Trouble.* New York: Scholastic.

Krashen, Steven. 2004. *The Power of Reading: Insights from the Research.* 2nd ed. Portsmouth, NH: Heinemann.

Lewison, Wendy Cheyette. 2010. *Silly Milly.* New York: Scholastic.

Linden, Eugene. 1999. "Can Animals Think?" *Time*, August 29. http://content.time.com/time/magazine/article/0,9171,30198,00.html.

Lobel, Arnold. 1970. *Frog and Toad Are Friends.* New York: HarperCollins.

Lord, Cynthia. 2006. *Rules.* New York: Scholastic.

MacLachlan, Patricia. 1985. *Sarah, Plain and Tall.* New York: Harper & Row.

McDonald, Megan. 2005. *Stink: The Incredible Shrinking Kid.* Somerville, MA: Candlewick Press.

Mere, Cathy. 2013. "Using Evernote for Forms and Templates." *Reflect & Refine: Building a Learning Community.* September 2. http://reflectandrefine.blogspot.com/2013/09/using-evernote-for-forms-and-templates.html.

Moser, Jason S., Hans S. Shroder, Carrie Heeter, Tim P. Moran, and Yu-Hao Lee. 2011. "Mind Your Errors: Evidence for a Neural Mechanism Linking Growth Mindset to Adaptive Post-Error Adjustments." *Psychological Science* 22 (12): 1484–89.

Newkirk, Thomas. 2008. "When Reading Becomes Work: How Textbooks Ruin Reading." http://www.nais.org/Magazines-Newsletters/ISMagazine/Pages/When-Reading-Becomes-Work.aspx.

———. 2011. *The Art of Slow Reading.* Portsmouth, NH: Heinemann.

———. 2013. *Speaking Back to the Common Core.* http://www.heinemann.com/shared/onlineresources/E02123/Newkirk_Speaking_Back_to_the_Common_Core.pdf.

NPR Staff. 2013. "Conservationists Call for Quiet: The Ocean Is Too Loud!" July 28. http://www.npr.org/2013/07/28/206362675/conservationists-call-for-quiet-the-ocean-is-too-loud.

Palacio, R. J. 2012. *Wonder*. New York: Alfred A. Knopf.

Pearson. 2014. *ReadyGEN. Reading Complex Text Grades K–5*. Professional Development Participant Workbook. Glenview, IL: Pearson.

Pennypacker, Sara. 2006. *Clementine*. New York: Hyperion Books for Children.

Peterson, John. 1972. *The Littles Give a Party*. New York: Scholastic.

Riordan, Rick. 2008. *The Titan's Curse: Percy Jackson and the Olympians*. New York: Hyperion Books for Children.

Rosenblatt, Louise. 2005. "The Acid Test for Literature Teaching." In *Making Meaning with Texts: Selected Essays*. Portsmouth, NH: Heinemann.

Rylant, Cynthia. 2007. *Mr. Putter & Tabby See the Stars*. Harcourt Books.

Sachar, Louis. 1987. *There's a Boy in the Girls' Bathroom*. New York: Random House.

———. 1992. *Marvin Redpost: Kidnapped at Birth?* New York: Random House.

———. 2000. *Marvin Redpost: A Magic Crystal?* New York: Random House.

Scholastic. 2013. *Kids and Family Reading Report*. 4th ed. http://mediaroom.scholastic.com/files/kfrr2013-noappendix.pdf.

Slobodkina, Esphyr. 1940. *Caps for Sale*. New York: HarperCollins.

Smith, Frank. 2004. *Understanding Reading*. 6th ed. Mahwah, NJ: Lawrence Erlbaum Associates.

Spilsbury, Richard. 2005. *The Great Outdoors: Saving Habitats*. Portsmouth, NH: Heinemann Library.

Spinelli, Jerry. 1997. *The Library Card*. New York: Scholastic.

———. 2002. *Loser*. New York: HarperCollins.

Twain, Mark. 1998. *The Adventures of Tom Sawyer*. Mineola, NY: Dover.

Wells, Gordon. 2009. *The Meaning Makers: Learning to Talk and Talking to Learn*. 2nd ed. Buffalo, NY: Multilingual Matters.

Welty, Eudora. 1983. *One Writer's Beginnings*. Cambridge, MA: Harvard University Press.

Zusak, Markus. 2007. *The Book Thief*. New York: Alfred A. Knopf.

INDEX